This book is published to accompany the
television series *Strictly Come Dancing*,
first broadcast on BBC1 in 2007.

10 9 8 7 6 5 4 3 2

Published in 2007 by BBC Books,
an imprint of Ebury Publishing,
A Random House Group Company.

Foreword by Bruce Forsyth and Tess Daly
Copyright © Woodlands Books Limited 2007
Main text by Alison Maloney
Copyright © Woodlands Books Limited 2007

BBC Books would like to thank Sam Donnelly,
Helen Bishop and the rest of the *Strictly Come Dancing*
production team for all their help in compiling this book.

Alison Maloney has asserted her right to be identified as
the author of this Work in accordance with the Copyright,
Designs and Patents Act 1988

The Random House Group Limited Reg. No. 954009

Addresses for companies within the Random House
Group can be found at www.randomhouse.co.uk

A CIP catalogue record for this book is available
from the British Library.

ISBN 978 1 846 07344 1

The Random House Group Limited makes every effort to
ensure that the papers used in our books are made from
trees that have been legally sourced from well-managed
and credibly certified forests. Our paper procurement
policy can be found on www.randomhouse.co.uk

Commissioning editor: Lorna Russell
Freelance editor: Emma Marriott
In-house editor: Eleanor Maxfield
Designer: Bobby Birchall, Bobby&Co
Production controller: Antony Heller

Colour origination by: Altaimage
Printed and bound in Italy by Graphicom Sri

Picture credits:
Pages 2–3 (curtain and disco ball – duplicated on
other pages), p.16–17 (flag), p.54, p.55 (balloons), p.56
and p.118 istockphoto.com; p.17 (middle) © ABC
Photographic Archives (Drew Lachey); p.16 (right)
INF/GoffPhotos.com (Heather Mills McCartney); p.57
(right) www.decuisine.co.uk (Ballroom Dancer Cake)
Barbie Doll is the RTM of Mattel Inc.; p.87 (top left)
and p.93 (top) PA Photos.

BBC Books would like to thank photographer Greg King
for the Dancersize photographs

All other photographs © BBC and © BBC Worldwide Ltd.
Series five images: photography by David Venni, directed
by Paul Anderson.

Strictly Come Dancing

The Official 2008 Annual

Alison Maloney

Contents

Foreword

When I first heard the idea for Strictly Come Dancing I couldn't stop laughing because I thought it would make a great comedy show! Throughout my years in show business, I have seen a lot of ballroom dancing and I imagined something like The Generation Game, with people falling over themselves all the time. How wrong I was! I didn't realise they would rehearse for four to five weeks before the show started and, with the excellent teaching they have from the professionals, I was surprised by how well the celebrities took to it. Some were still pretty bad, but most improve week upon week.

Bruce Forsyth

Ballroom dancers are among the most competitive people in sporting show business and in *Strictly Come Dancing* they manage to instil this into their celebrity partners. That's why it's become much more of a competition than I ever thought and, while it might start as a bit of fun, as the series goes on they really want to win.

The age span of the fans is quite incredible. It appeals to everyone from very young children to 90-year-olds. Even teenagers love it because, apart from the dancing, it's almost like a fashion show. You've got the fun with the judges, the competitiveness and the wonderful music. It's such a mixture of good things. I always knew that children would love the show because most of them have never seen dancing like it. The idea of men and women dancing around, together, in such a large space is entirely new to them, so it is bound to fire up their imagination.

As well as being great family entertainment, it has brought ballroom back. Ballroom dancing never stopped, it just hasn't been on television for over ten years. Now the dancers on our show, like Anton du Beke and Erin Boag, have become so well known by the public that they are stars in their own right. It has also encouraged people to have a go themselves. There are salsa clubs all over the country and people are signing up to schools and learning how to dance because they know it looks good and feels good. It's marvellous because for too many years it's been disco, disco, disco. I think when people dance they should hold each other. That's real dancing to me.

The popularity of the show means that stars are now keen to take part, whereas in the first series they were begging people to go on it. If you ask celebrities to learn to ballroom dance and perform live in front of ten million viewers, people are going to think very carefully about whether they want to do that! On the first show I saw Natasha Kaplinsky before she went on and she said, 'Oh, Bruce, can you get me off on the first week? I'm so nervous. I don't want to do this.' Within three or four weeks she was becoming a great dancer and by the end of the series she was the winner! People surprise themselves on the show. They don't know they can dance until they try it. It's a gift a lot of people have, but you only find out by doing it. Two of the series have been won by cricketers Darren Gough and Mark Ramprakash and I think they've been fantastic, as was Colin Jackson. Sportsmen have great control of their bodies because that's how they earn their living. It's only a matter of transferring that control in a new way and using the muscles they already have.

So many of the celebrities have impressed me with the way they improve after the first week of the television show. It's quite fascinating to watch. What the public still don't really understand is how much time they devote to it. The routines are only 90 seconds long but when you have to do them live, you have to spend hour upon hour learning the routine, and then perfecting it to make it better. The judges are great too. They can be a bit cruel at times but that means I can have a go at *them* and protect our celebrities! My own dance style has been tap and jazz, but I enjoy ballroom and my favourite dance is the American Smooth. It has so much feeling because you go against the beat and your partner has to feel that you are either going to pause ... move to the left ... or the right ... and she *has* to go with you. Let's just say I like to be in control!

Over the last five years Strictly Come Dancing has grown in popularity and has become an eagerly anticipated part of the year. People often tell me they miss it when it's not on and, believe me, I do too. The start of a new series is so exciting. The show has an electric atmosphere because it's live, the celebrities are dancing for the first time, and the outcome is totally unpredictable. They are always very nervous to start with and it's wonderful to be part of the process, watching them from their first tentative steps until they grow into competent and confident dancers.

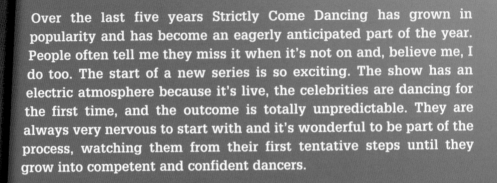

Tess Daly

It was great to see Mark Ramprakash win in series four because he had been on such a huge journey. He started off as possibly the shyest person we had ever had on *Strictly Come Dancing* – he wouldn't say boo to a goose! He always looked the part, of course, being so gorgeous, but he looked down at the floor all the time and Karen had to do all the talking. Then, before our eyes, his confidence grew and he turned into this incredible dancer. He came alive on the dance floor!

It's great fun to work on the programme and, because we go through the journey with all the celebrities, we get very close. That's why it's always sad to see them go and it can be difficult to control our emotions. Sometimes I have to try to keep my voice steady, and I've come close to shedding a tear on a few occasions. I was really sad when Peter Schmeichel left because he loved taking part. He told me that, since leaving professional football, he had missed the anticipation that built up before a game on a Saturday, but he got it back on *Strictly*. The whole training regime leading to that all-important performance on a Saturday was almost like being back at Old Trafford!

It's also hard when someone is voted out unexpectedly and so Spoony leaving so soon was a real shock. Had he been given another week or so to show what he could do, he could have easily got to the final. There are plenty of funny moments too. Chris Parker's Paso Doble in series one was hysterical and Colin and Erin's dance with the dolls in the final of series three was one of those moments I love, because it took everybody completely by surprise. And you should have seen how our jaws dropped when we found out the dolls were supposed to represent myself and Bruce.

The rehearsals just before the show are among the most thrilling moments for me, because we've seen the blood, sweat and tears that have gone into each routine and they have only 90 seconds to prove themselves on the night. You never know what the routine is going to be like and there are some wonderful surprises – like Colin Jackson doing the splits! The celebrities are amazing. I really admire them and the amount of dedication they put into it. They know roughly what they're in for but it still comes as a bit of shock when they find out how much training is actually required. They give it their all, and for some of them it is one of the biggest challenges they've ever undertaken.

If I wasn't presenting the programme I would love to be a contestant. I used to do a lot of dancing classes in my teens but to be trained to that level by a professional would be amazing. Mind you, I'm sure all the contestants are intimidated by the little dance that Brucie and I do at the top of the show. Bruce pretends not to notice when I tread on his toes!

I've been involved in *Strictly Come Dancing* since the beginning and I am as devoted to it as the fans that I talk to on the street. Even when I was off for six weeks, after having my daughter, Phoebe, I was cheering from the sidelines and chomping at the bit to get back. Phoebe will be three at the start of the next series and she already loves the show. She watches at home shouting, 'Daddy, there's Bruce.' She's a big Brucie fan! I feel very fortunate to be part of *Strictly Come Dancing* because it really is the greatest entertainment programme on television.

A to Z of Strictly Come Dancing

A is for Audience

The dedicated followers of the show bring the party atmosphere to the studio and liven up the evening. Their cheers and claps spur the dancers on but they also manage a good 'boo' – usually directed at Craig.

B is for Bruises

The tough training required for dancing leaves all the contestants black and blue. Natasha Kaplinsky may have been an outstanding dancer but she paid for the skills she learned – with three lost toenails and 27 bruises by the semi-final. Even the professionals are not immune. Karen Hardy, dance partner of series four winner Mark Ramprakash, fell and injured her knee while practising an Argentine Tango and was left with a 'cracking bruise'.

C is for Cape

As the Paso Doble is the dance of the matador, it often involves some impressive work with a cape. But while it is magnificent to watch, it can cause all kinds of problems in training. Chris Parker's hilarious Paso came after some even funnier cape training, while Mark Ramprakash spent hours mastering his technique and frequently ended up with a cape over his head. On the night it all went smoothly and matador Mark delivered what Bruno called 'a killer Paso Doble'.

D is for Dresses

The dazzling array of outfits created for the elegant female contestants have become stars in themselves. The clever creations of chiffon, sequins and beading have the ability to take our breath away before anyone dances a step. And, of course, there's always the odd one which we can bitch about too!

E is for Elephant

The charming Esther Rantzen, when describing her dancing style, commented, 'Think of a rather old, wrinkled elephant on skis and that's sort of my style.' Although she only made it to the third show of series two, Esther's first-night Waltz proved that E is also for Elegance.

F is for Fake Tan

A must for any ballroom dancer. It wouldn't do to be pasty for the Paso Doble when you could be tangoed for the Tango. Aled Jones, however, did not enjoy the experience of his first spray tan and complained, 'You're freezing my nipples!'

G is for Glitter Ball

The one thing that every couple has their eye on is the Strictly Come Dancing trophy. The mirrored ball epitomizes the glamour and glitz of the series and over the first four series has graced the mantelpieces of one newsreader, one actress and two cricketers.

H is for Heated Debates

With all four judges looking for different things, they frequently disagree and, on occasion, things can get a bit heated. Arlene's negative response to Louisa Lytton's Foxtrot had Craig and Bruno up in arms screaming, 'You are joking!', while Len told Bruno, 'You get on my wick sometimes.' After Clare and Brendan's Tango in series four, the fearsome foursome were arguing so much that Bruce had to blow a whistle to break it up!

I is for Incompatible

For every potential Fred and Ginger there's a Laurel and Hardy. Jill Halfpenny and Darren went together like strawberries and cream but David Dickinson and Camilla spent more time arguing than training, and the twelve-inch height difference between Jason Wood and Kylie in series one meant they couldn't be less like their pop-star namesakes. 'It's like Beauty and the Beast,' said Jason.

J is for Jokes

Bruce Forsyth may have more corn than a cereal factory but *Strictly Come Dancing* wouldn't be the same without his legendary jokes. Gags include: 'Ray (Mears) has demonstrated his Othello, impressed with his Romeo and even showed Camilla his Bottom!

K is for Knockout

The show's toughest moment for presenters and dancers alike is the ticking clock sound before they hear whether they are the latest to leave the show. The one thing all the celebrities have in common is the desire to win, so hearing their name announced can be like a punch in the stomach. And Tess gets pretty emotional too!

L is for Lifts

Illegal lifts are guaranteed to make steam come out of the ears of Len Goodman,

but that doesn't stop some of the dancers putting them in. Brendan is the worst offender and all the judges were furious with him after his Rumba with Clare King, which included several offending moves. Arlene awarded him a 'furious' four and Len railed, 'You're an absolute doughnut! I don't know why you do it. Brendan, you've got a screw loose.' So that told him!

M is for Music

Provided by veteran jazz musician Laurie Holloway in the first three series, the show's music is now the job of David Arch. The writer, arranger and musician has worked with such stars as Westlife and Alanis Morisette, as well as on the hit movie *Notting Hill*. His job is to produce a 90-second version of chosen songs that can be played live on the night. With songs ranging from the classics, such as 'Let's Face the Music', to modern hits, such as 'She Bangs' and 'I Don't Feel Like Dancin'', that's no mean feat!

N is for Nerves

The most experienced of performers can be floored by an attack of the jitters before their big Saturday night. Emma Bunton may think nothing of strutting her stuff in a pop video but she suffered terrible stage fright on *Strictly Come Dancing*. Likewise, Fiona Phillips and Jan Ravens found that nerves affected their performances on the night and even dancer Karen Hardy suffered a wobbly moment in series four.

O is for Olympians

Winning a gold at the Olympics is one thing, but it seems it doesn't prepare you for the rigours of *Strictly Come Dancing*. Olympic heroes Roger Black, Denise Lewis and Colin Jackson may have found the tough training a little easier than others, but even they ached in places they didn't know they had! As you'd expect, they thrived on the challenge and Colin and Denise excelled, both ending as silver medallists in the final.

P is for Props

Julian Clary had his maracas, Chris Parker had his hat and David Dickinson his red rose. Colin Jackson and Erin Boag came unstuck when they took the idea of props a little too far and ended up dancing with two puppets, to the horror of the judges.

Q is for Quentin

Introducing Quentin Willson to series two, Bruce quipped, 'Quentin has presented *Britain's Worst Drivers*, *Britain's Worst Homes* and *Britain's Worst Husbands* – and here he is dancing. Don't expect too much …' Little did he know how

prophetic his words were! Poor Quentin struggled on the floor and, after a terrible Cha Cha Cha, Craig dubbed him 'Britain's Worst Dancer' and Bruno commented, 'It was like watching a Reliant Robin keeping up with a Ferrari.'

R is for Relatives

Training can be a difficult and lonely experience for the celebrities but spirits are often boosted by the thought of their relatives watching their performances on Saturday nights. Louisa Lytton was thrilled to have her mum, dad and both grandmothers in the audience for her and Carol Smillie was buoyed up by the support of her husband and three children. Darren Gough took it one step further by taking partner Lilia home to Barnsley to meet his folks and Jill Halfpenny's mum did a lap of honour when her daughter picked up the trophy!

S is for Slips

Most couples suffer a few slips and falls in training but, for some, the worst nightmare comes true and they lose their footing during the live show. Recovery is everything. Matt Dawson slipped on the stairs in his American Smooth but still managed to impress the judges with a score of 34. Denise Lewis's Samba was almost scuppered by a slippery floor but she pulled it together after missing a step, prompting Bruno to say, 'You did miss a step but the floor is very slippery and it is very difficult to recover the way you did and carry on. Well done.'

T is for Tantrums

You may think they are the domain of five-year-olds but tantrums live on in the dance world. Athlete Roger Black stamped his foot like a spoiled toddler, while Jan Ravens stormed out on Anton when things got complicated. But that sort of behaviour isn't limited to the celebrities alone. Brendan refused to talk to Sarah after a Rumba went wrong and even laid-back Anton stormed off to his dressing room after his Samba with Patsy Palmer. Temper, temper!

U is for Unfair Dismissal

If you have never screamed at the telly when the latest couple are voted off at the end of the night, you haven't been paying attention. In series one Tess was left speechless after Claire Sweeney was knocked out in week five, despite high praise from the judges and a score of 32 for her Samba. Similarly, the other celebrities were shocked in series four when snake-hipped Spoony was voted out in the third week, despite being a favourite of the judges. Ray Fearon also fell victim to the public vote in week six, leading Len to comment, 'That's wrong!' as the results were announced. You public voters can be a cruel lot!

V is for Viennese Waltz

The Viennese Waltz holds a special place in the *Strictly Come Dancing* annals because it is a perfect dance for the

competitors to perform together in a group. That doesn't mean they don't get competitive. Brendan nearly came to blows with several fellow dancers during rehearsals for series one and each couple tried to outdo each other for their individual spot dance. But it's all good fun – and it always looks great!

W is for Waterworks

Whether it's Lesley Garrett's tears after elimination or Jan Ravens' tears of frustration, *Strictly Come Dancing* is never short of waterworks! Brendan reduced Sarah Manners to tears after a judges' savaging and the

X is for Xmas Specials

Hurray for the festive Foxtrot and the Jingle Bells Jive! The Xmas special gives *Strictly Come Dancing* fans an extra bite of the plum pudding as the top four celebrities for the previous series return to dance again, with an added bauble and a bit of tinsel. It also gives our dancing couples another chance to win, with the 2006 title going to Colin Jackson and Erin Boag.

panel had the same effect on several contestants, including Georgina Bouzova and Louisa Lytton. Even dancers Nicole and Camilla have shed a few tears and Colin Jackson welled up after getting three perfect tens for his Quickstep in the final.

Y is for Youngest

Lovely Louisa Lytton was only 17 when she whirled through the show like a breath of fresh air. Bruno was quite taken with the EastEnders star and gushed, 'What a gorgeous dancing little

baby doll you are!' Louisa easily held her own among the older celebrities. She and partner Vincent Simone made it to show ten before their Rumba sadly let them down.

Z is for Zoe

Despite achieving the highest scores across all four series in the Samba, Foxtrot, Tango and Rumba, Zoe Ball failed to win the final. A natural dancer, she and partner Ian Waite scored consistently good scores and the judges' votes on the final night put them at the top, with an amazing score of 76 out of 80. Sadly for Zoe, the public had fallen for Darren Gough and had been impressed by the grace of Colin Jackson, so Zoe was not to be the Belle of the Ball.

'I'll be getting down and dirty with the Latin and becoming a graceful princess with the ballroom '

Lovely Alesha Dixon is set to bring a little 'Mis-teeq' to series five. The R&B singer, turned MC, has threatened to turn up the heat with her Latin dances. 'My instinct says Latin will be my favourite as I have fire in my belly and am always moving,' she smiles. 'Latin is very fast-paced and fiery, so I think it will suit me. Then again, when I look at the ballroom they look like princesses, so I can't wait to have a go at that as well. I'll be getting down and dirty with the Latin and becoming a graceful princess with the ballroom.'

Alesha Dixon

Born in Welwyn Garden City, Alesha's career took off in 1999 as one third of the trio, Mis-Teeq. In 2001, Mis-Teeq released their debut album *Lickin' on Both Sides*, which featured the top ten hits 'All I Want', 'One Night Stand', 'B With Me' and double A single 'Roll On' and 'This Is How We Do It'. All the singles reached the top ten in the charts and the album went to number three in the UK album chart. Two years later, their second album, *Eye Candy*, produced the band's most successful single, 'Scandalous'. Used as the theme tune for *Catwoman*, starring Halle Berry, it reached the top ten in the UK, Ireland, New Zealand, Australia, Denmark as well as America.

After recording the single 'Shoo Shoo Baby' for the Disney film *Valiant*, the three girls announced they were going their separate ways and Alesha went on to present ITV's *CD:UK* and *CD:UK Hotshots*. Since then, she has returned to the studio to work on her solo album, due for release in 2008, and has signed up to make her first film, *Milestones*, opposite Brian Cox and Alex Kingston. And, before signing up as a contestant on *SCD*, she did a spot of judging celebrity performances herself, as a guest on *Comic Relief Does Fame Academy*.

Of course, as a pop star she is no stranger to dancing and actually started ballet when she was five. She gave it up after finding it was 'too quiet for me' and took up tap, but the cost of the lessons meant she had to drop out. Instead, she and her teenage friends made up dances at the school youth group. 'We got quite good and were entered into a national dance competition, Super Dance,' she recalls.

Having also choreographed some of Mis-Teeq's dance routines, *Strictly Come Dancing* should be a walk in the park, although Alesha doesn't think so. 'They were street dances, which are completely different,' she says. 'The thing I'm most worried about is not living up to my partner's expectations.' Unlike many of the other contestants, Alesha's main reason for signing up is to get fit. 'Before I became a musician I was very sporty and, ever since, I have wanted to get back to a good level of fitness,' she says. She also wants to make up for missing out on the dance lessons that her mum couldn't afford when she was growing up. 'I've always wondered how far I could have gone with it if I could have carried on, and how far I could have pushed myself.'

She will be dancing with Matthew Cutler

Smash hit shows inevitably lead to exports and *Strictly Come Dancing* is no exception. The format has now been adopted by 30 countries, including Australia and the US where, under the title *Dancing with the Stars*, it has proved a huge hit. The US version, which has been running since 2005, scored a major coup in its first season by attracting top stars like heavyweight boxing champion Evander Holyfield and Rod Stewart's ex-wife Rachel Hunter. It also poached our own Len Goodman and Bruno Tonioli to award the points, along with US dancer and choreographer Carrie Ann Inaba.

Dancing with the Stars

Evander Holyfield with UK dancer Karen Hardy.

Other than having just three judges, the format is almost indistinguishable from the BBC show and even the set looks familiar – right down to the mirror balls and velvet curtains. 'If you were blindfolded and taken to the one in America, you wouldn't know the difference – until the show begins,' explains Len. 'The audience are much more gregarious and outgoing in America. They boo and cheer and give standing ovations, and the dancing professionals teach more razzamatazz and go for the 'wow' factor much more, whereas the British professionals concentrate on the technique and the foundation of the dance.'

In 2007 *Dancing with the Stars* made a real impact on international headlines due to one particular participant – Heather Mills McCartney. Not only was she going through a very public divorce from one of the world's most famous musicians, Sir Paul McCartney, but she seemed to be at a distinct disadvantage when it came to dancing, in that she has a prosthetic leg! But she was nothing if not determined. Before long her partner, Jonathan Roberts, had her wowing the judges with ambitious routines that even included a back flip. 'Beyond any expectation!' Bruno gasped after the astounding display. 'You were on

> Obviously, I was fascinated to see how she'd cope dancing with one leg but after two weeks I didn't even think about the leg. I didn't notice. She was truly incredible and I really admired her **"**

warp drive tonight. Red-hot Heather – I can't believe what you did.'

Sadly for Heather, who lost her leg in a traffic accident in 1993, she was voted out in week six – a result which Len thinks was unfair. 'Heather was much better than I ever dreamt she could be,' comments Len. 'Obviously, I was fascinated to see how she'd cope dancing with one leg but after two weeks I didn't even think about the leg. I didn't notice. She was truly incredible and I really admired her. There were far worse dancers on the show but, like here, people vote for entertaining or popular people. For the first five weeks, only women were kicked out which is interesting because it's mainly women that vote. First, the model Paulina Porizkova went out, then it was the former Miss USA Shandi Finnessey. So it went on until Laila Ali, Mohammed Ali's daughter, was the only one left, but she was very good.'

Strangely, when the *Strictly* judges cross the pond, Len becomes Mr Nasty of the group – and Bruno shouts even more! 'In America, Bruno shouts a lot, and that gets on my nerves,' laughs Len. 'Carrie, who does it with us, is very sweet but she never says anything nasty to anyone. So I tend to be slightly harsher in America and Bruno shouts his head off at me. It gets right up my hooter – but only in a nice way!'

Rachel Hunter
The model and former wife of Rod Stewart appeared alongside Evander Holyfield in the first series of *Dancing with the Stars*. Tall and elegant as she may be, her dances with professional Jonathan Roberts didn't make the grade and she was eliminated in week four. She and Evander later appeared in the 2005 *Strictly Come Dancing* Christmas special.

Billy Ray Cyrus
The Country and Western singer behind the annoyingly catchy ditty 'Achy Breaky Heart' was paired with Karina Smirnoff and clung on to his part in the show for eight weeks. 'Billy Ray Cyrus was awful but kept getting voted back,' says Len. 'He was terrible!'

Drew Lachey
Former boy band star Drew Lachey and partner Cheryl Burke impressed judges and public alike to win the series two crown. The singer from 98 Degrees, and brother of Jessica Simpson's ex-hubby Nick, did the double in the final, getting a perfect score for each of their two dances. Other series winners so far are actress Kelly Monaco (season one), American football player Emmitt Smith (season three) and speed-skating champion Apolo Anton Ohno (season four).

Jerry Springer
The talk show host was partnered with Kym Johnson in season three and was popular with the viewers, if not the judges. Despite finishing in the bottom two on the leader board on four occasions, Jerry managed to scrape through to week seven before finally being eliminated.

Tatum O'Neal
The actress daughter of Ryan O'Neal and ex-wife of tennis legend John McEnroe is the only Oscar winner to have appeared on the show. She was paired with Nick Kosovich in season two and competed with the likes of George Hamilton, Tia Carrera (aka Mrs David Duchovny) and winner Drew Lachey. Tatum's success in the show was over way too soon, and she was the second person voted out.

Shilpa Shetty
Shilpa Shetty was a judge on the Indian version of the show. 'It was good because dancing has always been my forte,' says the Bollywood star. 'You have to be completely in control of what you say. You can't make a wrong assessment, you have to be judgemental and at the same time you can't be rude.' Has anyone told Craig!

Strictly

Stats

Ever wondered how much those ball gowns are worth, or how many crystals are used to make them sparkle? Here are the facts and figures that every fan should know.

For each series, the couples train for approximately *2447 hours*. Since *Strictly* started there has been *6672 hours* of dancing – that is *278 days* of continuous dancing!

Mark and Karen hold the record for the most hours danced by one couple - *312.5 hours* compared to Matt and Lilia's *209.25 hours* for the same series.

Up to series five, the dancers and celebrities have got through *236* bottles of fake tan – that's *47.2 litres* of fake suntan lotion!

The average Latin costume comes in with a price tag of *£1,500* while the ballroom dresses cost around *£2,000*. They are all made by dance-wear specialists Chrisanne, who hire them out to the BBC for the programme.

A dazzling *2.3 million* crystals have been sewn on to outfits by hand, and *855 metres* of fabric have gone into making the dresses.

The glamorous ladies in the first four series have worked their way through *139* sets of false eyelashes.

Perfect tens have been awarded by the judges on *25* occasions but there have been only four perfect scores of *40/40.* Although they failed to win series three, Zoe Ball and Ian Waite were awarded the most tens, with a total of six.

Dance schools across the country have reported a surge in attendance since *Strictly Come Dancing* started, with a considerable increase of men taking it up after Darren Gough's win in 2005.

In series four, over *12 million* votes were cast, and *13 million* viewers tuned into the final show to see Mark and Karen crowned 2006 *Strictly Come Dancing* Champions.

The much-coveted *Strictly Come Dancing* trophy weighs 3.2 kg and stands at *38 cm* tall and *28 cm* wide.

The costumes are very labour-intensive and *2,760* man-hours have been spent making the dresses.

The designers have made *500* costumes using *4.2 million* sequins – that's enough sequins for the combined populations of Birmingham and Manchester.

In the course of an evening a ballroom dancer can cover *8 kilometres* on the floor.

Ballroom dancing is a fantastic way to exercise and lose weight. For example, the Quickstep burns up to *480* calories an hour, whereas jogging only burns *390* calories and gardening *320* calories. And dancing is a lot more fun!

The Story of Series One
Strictly Come Dancing is Born

1 The calm before the storm

As eight eager celebrities gathered in the BBC studio, a new era in Saturday night entertainment dawned. The first series saw David Dickinson, Natasha Kaplinsky, Jason Wood, Martin Offiah, Lesley Garrett, Verona Joseph, Chris Parker and Claire Sweeney partnered with professional dancers to see who could cut the rug on the dance floor. Little did they know what they were letting themselves in for!

2 Claire's debut disappointment

With lead roles in stage musicals under her belt, many expected Claire Sweeney to burst onto the show as a clear winner. But the expectations were perhaps a little too much for the former *Brookside* star. Her Waltz with partner John Byrnes was a disappointment to Bruno. 'Claire, I'm sorry,' he said. 'You're a dancer. I expect much more from you. Boring.'

3 Blood, sweat and tears

The tears and tantrums began before the couples had performed a single chassé. Natasha decided she didn't want to do the show at all and shouted at the cameraman. Meanwhile, David Dickinson was proving difficult, arguing with partner Camilla Dallerup throughout the training. 'The first beat is two,' he moaned at an exasperated Camilla. 'Why didn't you tell me that?'

4 Lesley hits a high note

Lesley Garrett hit a high note with the judges in show two – literally. The excitable singer managed a sizzling Rumba after saying, 'If I can pretend to be to be this incredibly hot Latin woman instead of a housewife and mum from North London, I might pull it off.' She was so ecstatic after her performance that she gave partner Anton du Beke a smoochy kiss and demonstrated her vocal skills with an ear-piercing note!

5 Kylie and Jason

Camp comedian Jason Wood struggled with the elegance of the Waltz in week one and found the butch Rumba difficult in week two. 'Jason was a little bit shocked,' explained partner Kylie Jones. 'I don't think he's used to having his hands all over a woman's body.' The height difference of over a foot hardly helped matters and Craig awarded him a score of two. Not surprisingly, the couple were the first to be knocked out.

6 Natasha and Brendan's Quickstep triumph

Elsewhere, Natasha was at her lowest point in training but managed to wow the judges with her Quickstep, getting a score of 31, while Chris called it 'the most stupid dance I've ever done in my life'.

David and Camilla

Lesley and Anton

Verona and Paul

Martin and Erin

Natasha and Brendan

Christopher and Hanna

7 Martin dances through the pain

Martin Offiah's Jive training hit a huge hitch in the third week, when he sprained his ankle at a charity football match. The beefy rugby player was carted off to the physiotherapist and complained, 'It's killing me, man!' But you can't keep a good man down and he smiled through the pain, saying, 'On Saturday night I'm going to forget about it and go for it!'

8 David gets thorny in a Tango

David and Camilla continued to squabble their way through Tango training, with David complaining, 'You're not exactly explaining it to me simply!' At her wit's end, Camilla replied, 'I'm trying, David,' while clearly thinking he was the one who was trying – very! The antique expert finished with a rose between his teeth after asking in training, 'You don't think this is a bit poncey, do you?' Sadly David and his famous 'jazz hands' were voted out.

9 Brendan's Foxtrot fury

A tired and tetchy Brendan got so frustrated with Natasha's attempts at the Foxtrot that he stormed out of the training room and shouted, 'I don't want it recorded. Turn it off!' at the cameraman. 'I'm basically not coping,' he admitted. 'I'm not sleeping.' A day off and a good night's sleep and the pair were back on track, delivering a stunning routine and scoring a massive 35 from the judges.

10 Martin's the butt of the joke

Elsewhere things were getting personal as Martin Offiah's Foxtrot received general praise from the judges before Craig added, 'Your butt sticks out too much.' During training for the following week's Samba, the remark had clearly hit home. 'I'm going to shake my butt right in Craig's face,' said the defiant sportsman. 'He said I have a big butt, so I'm going to use it.'

11 Paul and Verona's passionless Paso Doble

Claire Sweeney and partner John Byrnes pulled off a blistering Paso Doble which had Bruno gasping, 'Claire is quite the sexiest bull I have ever seen.' Sadly for John's keenest rival, Paso Doble expert Paul Killick, Verona's dance didn't hit the spot with all the judges. Although Len said he could 'smell the blood and the Spanish onions'. Craig thought it had 'no passion whatsoever', and it seems the public agreed. Paul and Verona were voted out.

12 Arlene's murder accusation

Chris Parker and his partner, Hanna Karttunen, went all Austin Powers in week five – but the *EastEnders* star failed to find his mojo. The routine was more spoof than Samba. 'Oh dear,' muttered an appalled Arlene. 'Murder on the dance floor! You murdered the Samba tonight.' Poor Chris was mortified. The sad look on his face must have touched the nation's hearts – despite a shocking score of 15, the couple managed to stay in the competition.

Claire and John

Jason and Kylie

The Story of Series One Continued

13 A perfect moment

Natasha and Brendan's sexy Samba won them lavish praise from the judges, and Natasha was stunned when Arlene awarded her the first ten of the series. Lesley's shimmies came in for special praise from Bruno and had Bruce chuckling, 'I'm glad you mentioned the shimmies. I couldn't take my eyes off them!'

22

14 That's got to hurt!

Claire and John shimmied their way through an impressive Samba, which included the actress and singer performing the splits. By the look on her face, it wasn't the easiest thing she'd ever done! The judges were impressed. 'Very hot wiggle,' said Bruno, while Arlene commented that they were 'dancing from the soul. You swept the floor.' Sadly the public disagreed and Claire and John danced their last dance to the strains of 'Bye Bye Baby'.

15 Turning tables

By week six, Natasha had the dancing bug so badly she started telling Brendan what to do. Never a good move! After putting up with a bit of earache, Brendan finally cracked and complained, 'We're not doing any Rumba, Natasha.' When it came to the performance it seems the judges agreed and Len criticised the couple for not including 'one step of basic'. The elegant pair proceeded to prove him wrong by dancing the steps again.

16 Cape fear

Chris Parker struggled to get to grips with the cape work in the Paso Doble and gave a performance that was more madman than matador. 'I'm speechless,' said Arlene, and then went on to prove she was anything but. 'Let us not forget that this is a ballroom dancing competition and the Caped Crusader doesn't make it by running around the floor!'

Christopher & Hanna

17 Offiah goes out

Having admitted that he finds dancing more mentally challenging than rugby, Martin met his match in the Quickstep and got some of the steps wrong. 'The Quickstep is fast and furious,' commented Craig. 'And that was the lamest Quickstep I've ever seen.' The Cha Cha Cha didn't help matters and Martin and Hanna ended with a score of 48 for the two dances. Although Chris and Hanna were bottom with a measly 37, the public saved Chris once again and Offiah went out.

18 Lesley's left hook

The semi-finals saw the pressure pile up and lovely, bubbly Lesley boiled over. Struggling with the Jive, she told Anton, 'It doesn't have to be this complicated,' to which he responded, somewhat immaturely, 'Blah, blah, blah.' His frustrated dance partner flipped and slapped Anton round the face before storming out. Temper, temper!

Within image 1 (score display):
JUDGE 1 JUDGE 2 JUDGE 3 JUDGE 4 TOTAL
9   10

19 — The knives are out for Chris

Having miraculously made it through to the semi-final, Chris found his lack of dancing ability was beginning to be noticed. 'Chris Parker, sorry mate, but you can't dance to save your life,' commented Brendan. Craig went further with his criticism after a weak Rumba. 'You cannot dance,' he told the young soap star. 'And you have an annoying habit of licking your lips all the time!' So that told him.

20 — The diva departs

Natasha and Brendan finished top of the leader board with a score of 35 for their passionate Paso Doble, and their place in the final was secured. But there was a shock departure as Chris and Hanna held on for dear life, and a score of 29, against Chris and Hanna's miserable 16, failed to save Lesley from the chop.

21 — Chris and Hanna take precautions!

As the final approached, Hanna put her life in Chris's hands while they practised some lifts. Not wanting to end the series with a broken arm, however, Hanna borrowed a crash mat for training. It proved a necessary precaution and she lived to tell the tale!

22 — Do you love me?

For their Jive, Chris and Hanna chose the Blues Brothers' track 'Do You Love Me?' and Chris stole a line from the song to show he was psyched-up to win. 'I'm back to let you know, Craig,' he said, 'that I can really shake 'em down!' In fact, the Jive proved he still couldn't dance that well and the judges didn't love him at all. His Waltz was criticised as 'flat-footed' by Arlene and Craig called the opening of his Jive 'naff'. The couple also slipped in an illegal lift that didn't do them any favours.

23 — You lift me up

After a triumphant Quickstep and a sexy Samba, bad boy Brendan came into his own for the freestyle dance. With the rules thrown out of the window, Brendan could do as many lifts as he liked and he stunned the crowd when he lifted the beautiful newsreader right above his head. 'You were so close to dropping her,' said Craig. Bruno loved the 'spectacular lifts' and told the couple, 'That *Dirty Dancing* lift is so difficult to do and it's incredible what you have done.'

24 — Brendan and Natasha smile

After eight weeks of pure magic, and some very strange voting, the public finally came to their senses. Len, who had been frustrated by the public's decisions, gave one final plea, saying, 'Don't moan if you don't phone.' Over a million people did just that and Natasha and Brendan became the first King and Queen of *Strictly Come Dancing*.

Series One
Winner's Story
Natasha Kaplin

From the instant Natasha and Brendan stepped on to the floor, they looked like they were made to dance together. But Natasha's heart was definitely not in it. 'The only thing that's going to get me out of this now is to break an ankle,' moaned the breakfast news presenter on the eve of the first show. 'It really is tomorrow night – and I'm petrified.'

Looking back, she admits she was hoping her BBC *Breakfast* bosses would ban her from taking part. 'It filled me with dread and horror and gave me countless sleepless nights,' she recalls. 'The thought of stepping out on the dance floor and putting my credibility at risk was a massive fear for me. I was genuinely phobic about it. I tried to get out of it, step off kerbs and break my ankle – anything but do the show.'

Even when she began to enjoy the dancing, and the judges started to lavish praise on her, the worry of damaging her image meant she found it hard to relax. 'Those Saturday nights were agony,' she says. 'I've never come closer to panic attacks. Even when I talk about it now, I can feel my breath shortening and my chest getting tight. I found stepping out of my suit and putting on a dress and saying, "Look at me" genuinely traumatic. And then, to go on and win it, that was ridiculous, a mistake.'

Natasha also found the wardrobe required for the show a little hard to handle. 'It was all too girlie for my liking,' she says. 'When they were trying to convince me, two of the costume designers came to see me, and they brought dancers' dresses with them. I got more and more quiet. I almost burst into tears.

Although they looked great together, the attitudes of Natasha and dance partner Brendan Cole could not have been further apart at the beginning. While Natasha declared that she would be in the show for two weeks only, the ever-competitive Brendan argued, 'That's funny because I thought I'd be in it for the whole eight weeks.' After Craig described their first routine as 'dull, dull, dull!', Natasha was still in the doldrums and seemed to be dragging Brendan down with her. But by week three, Brendan's patience had run out and he decided it was time to put his foot down. 'Gentleman Jim is out the window!' he declared. 'The caveman is here.' 'He was gentle and polite at first,' jokes Natasha. 'But after a few weeks he turned into a bit of a brute.'

On Natasha ...

The brutal treatment seemed to work and Natasha threw herself into their next dance, which Len called 'the best Jive of the night', before penalising the couple for an illegal lift put in by bad boy Brendan. Finally, Natasha admitted she had caught the dancing bug. 'I'm in love with ballroom dancing!' she said and proved it in week five by getting the first ten of the series for a sizzling Samba – despite an undetected head-butt from Brendan. 'Natasha, you amaze me,' commented Len. 'That was a delight to watch.'

By the time the semi-final came around, Natasha's amazing transformation was complete. The couple's Waltz and Paso Doble earned them a combined score of 71 out of 80 and Arlene told Natasha, 'You are no

> **'The sense of achievement is like nothing else I've experienced.'**

longer a celebrity, you are a professional dancer!' With Lesley Garrett and Anton du Beke voted out at the end of the semi, the final was something of a foregone conclusion. Rival Chris Parker, although popular with the viewers, was hardly Fred Astaire when it came to the dance moves. That didn't stop Natasha spending the final week putting in her phone votes for the *EastEnders* star! And before the final dance-off, Natasha decided the time had come to swallow a little humble pie. 'I've been going around apologising to everyone, especially Brendan, because I was so horrible at the beginning,' she said.

Despite a microphone tangle in the Samba, which caused Natasha to lose a little of her usual composure and timing, the couple stunned the judges with their freestyle dance – and Brendan finally got to show off his lifts without being penalised! 'I can't tell you how many times I've been dropped this week,' joked Natasha, whose training had also seen her lose three toenails and suffer 27 bruises and several burn marks from fishnet tights! But the pain was forgotten as the 32-year-old presenter became the proud recipient of the first ever *Strictly Come Dancing* trophy. 'The sense of achievement is like nothing else I've ever experienced,' she said.

Fans of *Coronation Street* might feel a shiver down their spines when Brian Capron dances the Paso Doble. His portrayal of sinister serial killer Richard Hillman had the nation on the edge of their seats, and his exit has gone down as one of the most memorable storylines in the history of the soap.

Brian Capron

Away from the cobbles, Brian is a happily married man with three children and he had agreed to do *Strictly Come Dancing* to please his loved ones. 'All my family and friends are huge fans of the show and my mother-in-law is crazy about it!' he explains. 'I would never have thought about doing it but, out of all the reality shows, I think it is the most genuine and a real challenge.'

Brian, who lives in Brighton with wife Jacqueline, has an acting career which spans 35 years. His breakthrough came in 1980 when he landed the role of woodwork teacher Dan 'Hoppy' Hopwood in children's drama *Grange Hill*, where he stayed for three years. After a series of smaller parts, including six different characters in *The Bill*, Brian played Jerry Mackenzie in *EastEnders* from 1993 to 1994.

In 2001, he strolled on to the set of *Coronation Street* as Richard Hillman, a respectable financial advisor and the man of Gail's dreams. From there, he turned into a fraudster and

He will be dancing with Karen Hardy

eventually a killer, bumping off several *Street* residents, before attempting to murder his new screen family, the Platts. His exit in 2003 earned him awards for Best Actor, Best Exit and Villain of the Year at the British Soap Awards.

Since then, Brian has starred in the television series *Where The Heart Is* and has also tried out his dancing feet in the musicals *Guys and Dolls* and *The Rocky Horror Show*. Neither experience, he reckons, is likely to help him on *SCD*. 'I had to do the Time Warp with the rest of the cast in *The Rocky Horror Show* which was great and very funny,' he says. 'And I did a little dancing for *Guys and Dolls*, which was the first time I'd danced on stage. I think I was hopeless but I managed to blag it.'

The first night didn't go quite as he'd planned, however. 'I ran out on stage but I was doing the wrong dance,' he laughs. 'I was lucky, though, because no one in the audience seemed to notice.'

The 60-year-old soap star does admit to some training in ballroom – when he was 11. He went to classes for one term but he was pretty useless. This time around, he is looking forward to the Latin, because he likes the bright costumes, and he is especially fond of the Salsa. 'I'll be more than happy to make it through the first round but I would like to win it, especially for my gay friends, who are the biggest fans of the show,' he says.

His own dancing hero is somewhat unconventional. 'I'm hoping that this competition will help me to compete with my break-dancing son, Louis, because I love Christopher Walken's dancing in the Fatboy Slim video for "Weapon of Choice". Maybe, after taking part in the show, I could dance like that.' Now what would Len Goodman say to that?

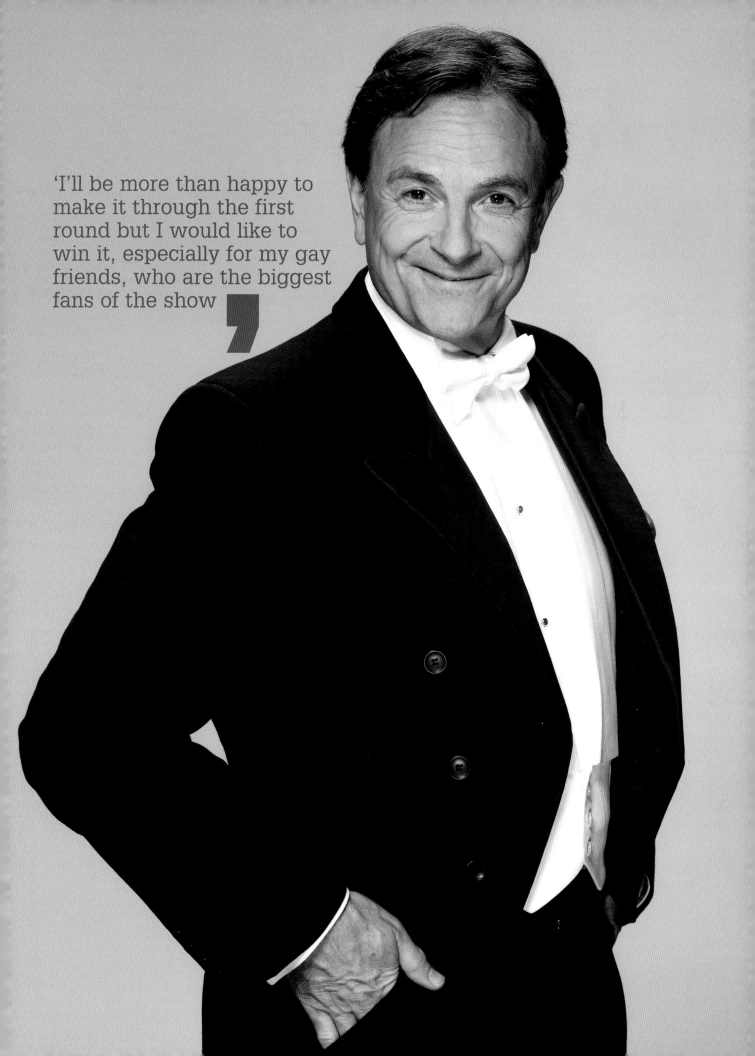

'I'll be more than happy to make it through the first round but I would like to win it, especially for my gay friends, who are the biggest fans of the show'

The Fearsome Foursome

Strictly Come Dancing came into Len Goodman's life as something of a sixtieth birthday present. Having been asked to join the show, he celebrated his landmark day while making the pilot. 'It was a marvellous present,' he says. 'And I'm glad I was asked when I was getting on a bit because if I'd been asked in my twenties, I'd have thought I was a superstar and gone all Hollywood!'

Since then, Len has become a household name and has won the hearts of the nation with his generous approach to the celebrities' efforts on the dance floor. 'I'm not a particularly nice person, you know,' he laughs. 'I just find it quite hard to be really nasty because I admire those celebrities. They are completely out of their comfort zone, away from what they are used to doing, and the standard is amazing. When we first started, we thought they could train for a couple of hours twice a week, but the commitment and amount of effort they put in is astounding. And often they have their proper jobs to do too, whether it's reading the news or singing, so their training has to be fitted in around their schedules. That's why it gets on my nerves when Craig gives them a two. I think they should get a two just for turning up!'

Len, a former British Champion who now runs two dance schools in Kent, grew up in the East End and dreamed of being a footballer. Coming to dance relatively late, at nineteen, he worked as a docker before a football injury led him to a dance studio. He admits that his motives were more about meeting girls than picking up the Quickstep. 'A friend of mine used to disappear every Wednesday night but never told us where,' the ballroom expert recalls. 'Eventually, I wheedled out of him that he went to a dance class and was ashamed of himself. Then he said, "Len, it's fantastic. There are four boys up there and 60 girls!" When you're eighteen, virtually your whole objective in life is to meet girls, so I went with him, and of course I loved it. There were a handful of boys and all these gorgeous girls and, once I'd learned a bit, they all wanted to dance with me, so I was the king of the castle.'

Soon Len was partnering the daughter of the dance studio's owner, which brought him to the attention of the head honcho himself. 'She'd been dancing since she was two, and we got really friendly. Then the owner thought we had potential so he started to coach us to compete. By the time I was in my late twenties, I won the British Championships at Blackpool. At this point I decided my motivation was more about earning a

Len

living than becoming the greatest ever ballroom dancer, so I retired. I then opened my dancing school.'

Thirty years later, Len is back in the spotlight as the world's most famous

ballroom judge. But not everyone he meets agrees with his scores on the night. 'If ever they decide to replace us judges, they only have to go any queue of women at a supermarket checkout,' he chuckles. 'They're all experts! They come up to me and say, "How could you have given so-and-so a seven? They danced beautifully!"' But with a split-second decision to make on the show, Len admits that he has got it wrong in the past. 'I did critique wrongly once, with Martin Offiah,' he confesses. 'We don't see the dances prior to everyone else, and you have to give your mark as soon as they finish dancing, so you only have three or four seconds.' He continues, 'When I watched Martin's Cha Cha Cha again, I thought I'd marked him down. At the end of the season I admitted to him that I should have given him a higher mark, and he was very gracious about it.'

The runaway success of *Strictly Come Dancing* has led to a huge resurgence of interest in dance schools like Len's, with more and more people of all ages signing up for classes. It's a trend that our head judge is delighted to see. 'It's amazing!' he says. 'Almost every dance studio around the world has had a fantastic increase in new people joining. One of the things I love about the show is that it has got people out of the house dancing. If you're married or with a partner, it's something you can do with them. If you are on your own, it's an opportunity to meet new people, so it's been great. And when you see Darren Gough or Mark Ramprakash dancing, it even makes young men think that it's not such a sissy thing after all.'

'At the end of the season I admitted to him that I should have given him a higher mark, and he was very gracious about it'

The success of the Saturday night show, which attracts over 13 million viewers and has been exported around the world, has exceeded all expectations – not least those of Len himself. 'When I first got asked to do this, I said, "I can't see the professionals being able to produce much of a standard. I think it will only last one series." How wrong I was!' Which just goes to show that even Len Goodman can't be right all the time.

It Takes Two

Claudia

Each new series of *Strictly Come Dancing* means months of work for Claudia Winkleman – and she couldn't be happier. The 35-year-old presenter, who fronts sister programme *It Takes Two*, is one of the show's biggest fans and is delighted to be coming back for series five. 'I'd cry if they didn't ask me,' she enthuses. 'I love it. I'm very excited. *It Takes Two* is a lot of fun to work on and there's lots of giggling.'

Since the second series of *Strictly Come Dancing*, Claudia has followed the highs and lows of each contestant and watched hours of training videos in order to bring a fresh perspective to her BBC2 show, five nights a week. Understandably, she gets quite attached to the celebrities taking part and has also become very close to the dancers. 'I love all the dancers because for four months of the year I see them more than I see my family,' she says. 'I'll be having supper with Darren and Lilia and learning more about Foxtrot steps than my son's geography class!'

Claudia even likes the judges and gets on fantastically with the meanest of them all, the merciless Craig Revel Horwood. Contestants may cringe at their caustic comments but, she reveals, they are not as bad as they seem away from the camera. 'They're not stern at all,' she explains. 'They're fantastic. I love Craig. He's so funny he makes me cry with laughter.'

After a few series of *It Takes Two*, Claudia is something of a *Strictly Come Dancing* expert – but you're not likely to catch her attempting a Tango any time soon. 'I'd never do it because I'd be rubbish,' she laughs. 'I like a bit of disco dancing and I won a robotics contest when I was 13, but I can't do ballroom dancing to save my life!' And she has nothing but admiration for those who throw their diamanté hats into the ring. 'I would be terrified because you are dressed in an outfit you would never wear, doing moves that you would never do, in front of millions of viewers. The whole thing is terrifying, so hats off to them. They're very brave.'

Amazingly, not one celebrity has actually bowed out on the night. 'Almost everybody cries at some point,' reveals Claudia. 'People get ill, can't eat, get their toes broken because they are training so hard, or are paralysed with nerves, but they all manage to carry on.' Claudia continues, 'Fiona Phillips was terrified and Emma Bunton was really scared. I remember talking to lovely Mark Ramprakash early on and he said, "I'm going to do badly; I'm going to be rubbish; I'm not going to be able to do it." And he went on to win series four!'

Although not all the celebrities taking part become skilled dancers, some of the less likely candidates can surprise everyone. 'Darren Gough just came along in leaps and bounds,' recalls Claudia. 'I think people love to see that. It's interesting that sportsmen have done so well, because they have that competitive nature and the determination not to fail.'

As well as meeting the celebrities, Claudia spends time with the families who come along to support them. 'Their families get so involved,' she says. 'My favourite was Mark Ramprakash's daughter, who said, "Cricket's boring. We like it when you do dancing!"'

Claudia watches avidly at home with husband Kris and their two young children. 'We are always trying to predict what the judges will score for each dance, so we're both shouting "eight" and "seven" at the telly. The kids have no idea what's going on!'

'I like a bit of disco dancing and I won a robotics contest when I was 13, but I can't do ballroom dancing to save my life!'

If Mum is anything to go by, the children are bound to develop a passion for the sequins and pearls of the Saturday night show themselves. 'I think there are so many levels of appeal,' says the devoted fan. 'There are the judges, who are magnificent, and there's Bruce and Tess, the best double act on the screen. Watching celebrities do something that they are not used to doing is fascinating, and it's so hard, so all-encompassing.' Finally, there's the glamour. 'You put on a huge amount of beading, high-heeled shoes, a headdress, and loads of make-up, and then dance on a shiny wooden floor. It doesn't get much more glamorous than that!'

apply it because it has to look spotless. We used to be more casual and say, "It'll be fine," but now you can't get away with anything.'

The rehearsals throughout the day can be gruelling affairs and Sarah reveals that some of the celebrities can come back a little sweaty. 'The dancers are obviously used to lots of exercise so they are okay, but some of the celebrities aren't so used to it, so they sweat a lot,' she says. 'But they don't smell, as far as I know. The only smell you get in the make-up room is fake tan.'

Having worked on the make-up for Bruce and Tess in previous series, Sarah then took over the look for dancers and celebrities in series four, and set about trying to change a few things. 'I wanted to try to make it a bit more modern,' she reveals. 'I work a lot in fashion and I wanted to give it a slightly fresher look.' One thing she is trying to tone down is the famous fake tan. 'I'm trying my hardest to wean them off it,' she laughs. 'Last year I was determined they wouldn't look so orange and the celebrities are often a bit wary of the fake tan to start with but after a few weeks of dancing, they want more! It's a constant battle. And the male celebrities are just as bad as the women. If you are dancing with someone who's incredibly brown, whether you're male or female, you want to be the same. When I'm working on the show, even I get through a bottle a week!'

Although Sarah and her team, who number nine at the beginning of each series, work hard to create new looks, there are some things that are dictated by the dances themselves. 'Each dance has a specific style,' explains Sarah. 'With ballroom, for example, we have to see the nape of the neck and the dancers are quite rigid, especially the guys. Latin is freer and much sexier, so the hair can be worn down. We look at the dance and who the dancers are. If you have someone really funky, like Louisa Lytton, you don't want to make her look like she's in her fifties. You also consider hair-type, what they're wearing, and the music they're

dancing to, and then you try to marry all of that together. Once you get the look, you make sure they are happy with it – especially the dancers because they really feel that the hair, make-up and clothes are a big part of what they're doing. If that's wrong, they don't feel they can perform quite so well.'

Strangely, the styles which take the most work are the ones for the Latin dances, when the hair is flowing freely. 'The worst is a curly style on someone who has straight hair because you curl it and then they get into dress and make-up and it's fallen out,' she says. 'If hair is up, it stays there but if hair is down it actually takes more re-doing throughout the day.'

As with the wardrobe department, the hair and make-up team live in fear of something going wrong on the night. And there have been one or two occasions which might have resulted in some bitten nails in the wings. 'I live in dread of someone doing a Paso Doble and a hairpiece flying off,' laughs Sarah. 'It hasn't happened to me yet!' She adds, 'There was one week in series three when Emma Bunton's hair extensions got caught in Darren's microphone and it had actually pulled out loads of her hair. I was slightly mortified but there was nothing I could do. Every Saturday night, we sit there with bated breath. Everyone else is watching the dancing and we are watching the eyelashes and the hairstyles!'

'*Strictly Come Dancing* is a show that you watch and smile the whole way through, and I want to make people smile when I dance '

As a former international gymnast, Gabby Logan is bound to have some surprise moves up her sleeve. The glamorous sports presenter has long been a fan of *Strictly Come Dancing* and has always wanted to try it herself. 'The show is amazing,' she says. 'It gets better every year. I think it will be a challenging experience but it also looks so much fun. I'm very excited about taking part.'

Gabby Logan

In fact, she was so excited she persuaded her dance-shy husband, Scottish rugby player Kenny Logan, to join her on the show, making them the first husband and wife celebrities to compete. Watching at home will be their two-year-old twins, Rueben and Lois – who might just wonder why Mummy and Daddy aren't dancing with each other! The couple met at a London nightclub but Gabby says the one and only time they have danced together was at their 2001 wedding. 'He was so nervous and hated dancing in front of everyone.'

As well as being married to a sportsman, Gabby has sport in the blood, as the daughter of footballer Terry Yorath. As a teenage gymnast she represented Wales at the 1990 Commonwealth Games in Auckland, gaining eighth place in rhythmic gymnastics. And when she is not working or looking after the twins, she is running half-marathons or practising yoga!

With a competitive streak that has made her something of a high achiever, Gabby might prove hard to beat. She has succeeded in the male-dominated world of sports presenting and, in 2002, became the first woman to present a live terrestrial football match when covering Chelsea v Spurs. She has also won a host of awards, including two Sports Personality of the Year awards from TRIC (Television and Radio Industries Club).

She will be dancing with James Jordan

Strictly Come Dancing is not the first time she has stepped out of her comfort zone for a public performance. Her impression of Sharleen Spiteri for a 2002 *Stars in their Eyes* was so impressive that the Texas singer sent flowers to congratulate her. Although Gabby would like to win, she is content just to put a smile on a few faces.

'*Strictly Come Dancing* is a show that you watch and smile the whole way through, and I want to make people smile when I dance,' she says. 'And I hope I come away knowing how to dance.'

But that's not the only thing she's looking forward to. The ever-glamorous presenter can't wait to get her hands on those frocks! 'I want to stay long enough to wear all my dresses,' she reveals. Gabby is also looking forward to the Latin dances. 'I like the quick movements of the Latin because it's quite a sexy dance style, but I can also appreciate the elegance of ballroom.'

But, judges, beware! Feisty Gabby might be too hot to handle. 'I hate criticism,' she admits. 'But I am looking forward to a good argument!'

WARM UP AND

Warm up

Start with a slow warm up. Any dance will do nicely. Cold muscles suddenly put to work are more likely to become damaged than ones that have been warmed up properly. Warming up will gradually increase your heart and breathing rates, increasing the flow of oxygen and nutrients to your muscles before you begin to work them hard. In addition, your joints secrete more synovial fluid and become less stiff. The body is properly adapting to the demands of exercise.

Stretch

Between dances, do a bit of stretching. You can do some beneficial stretches unobtrusively, even when dressed nicely. Slowly bend down, reaching for your toes. Hang forward, counting to 15. Let gravity do the stretching. Don't force the stretch. Then lean over to each side, making a giant letter 'C', again for 15 seconds. Then bend your knees and

STRETCH

shift from side to side, stretching the groin muscles. Lastly, roll your shoulders around a couple of times. Now you're ready for more vigorous dancing!

Drink lots of water

During the dance, be sure to drink lots of water. Without enough water, your body doesn't function optimally. You 'wilt', much like a plant that needs water. Avoid alcohol, which is a diuretic, stealing water from your body. The same goes for coffee or soda with caffeine.

Increase your activity gradually

In general, do not increase the intensity or duration of your dancing more than 10% in a week. Do not increase both intensity and duration during the same week. Allow your body to recover properly and adapt slowly to improved performance levels.

Strictly DANCERSIZE

Do eight of everything unless otherwise specified

CHA CHA CHA

If you are a beginner, the Cha Cha Cha is the best one to start with, as it is the easiest dance to follow. The Cha Cha Cha hails from the 1940s, when orchestras slowed down the Rumba to give those less proficient at the fast-paced steps a chance. The origin of the name is under some debate: some say it is named after a type of Haitian bell and others say it's from the sound made by sandals slapping on the dance floor.

There's a lot of hip action and a bit of bump and grind, so it's great for working the waist, thighs and bottom. Just make sure you get those hips moving!

Move 1
The basic time step

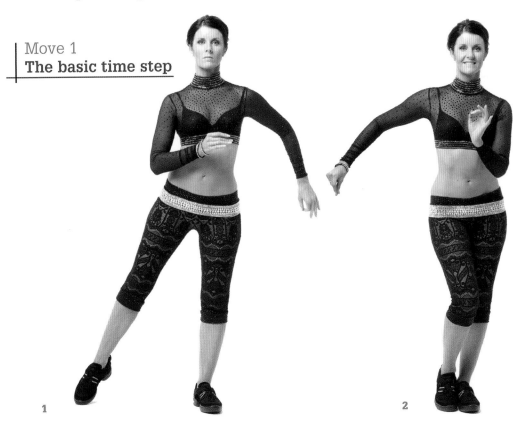

1   2

There are few exercises as effective as dancing and it has the added advantage of being fun. Here are some exercises you can learn in the privacy of your own home – just put on some music and dance to your heart's content!

Think 'left, right, Cha Cha Cha, right, left, Cha, Cha, Cha.'
- Start with your weight on the left foot and right toe pointed outwards, as if you are leaning on a bar **(1)**
- Bring right leg over to touch the left, with your weight on your left hip **(2)**
- Step to the left, so that your feet are hip distance apart **(3)**
- Close feet and step to the left, then close quickly (Cha Cha Cha) **(4)**
- Point left leg to the side, with weight on right **(5)**
- Repeat in the opposite direction

3   4   5

Move 2
Cha Cha Slide

1   2   3   4   5

- Start as in step 1 **(1)**
- Bring the right foot into the left, with a slight hip swivel **(2)**
- Bend the left knee over the right in a swivelling movement (Cha Cha) **(3)**
- Step to the left **(4)** and repeat Cha Cha movement **(5)**
- Slide to the right, with right arm straight up and the other at 90 degrees
- Repeat in the opposite direction

Move 3
Cuban Breaks

1   2   3

- Start with arms outstretched, leaning on your slightly bent left leg, with right foot behind, hip distance apart **(1)**
- Bring your right leg across your knee, with both knees bent **(2)**
- Return to start position, with hip to the right and right toe pointed **(3)**
  Do in sets of eight on each side, starting with one set and working up to three

CHA CHA CHA

Move 4
New York

- Start with arms outstretched and body turned to the side, with right foot behind the left (1)
- Step in to the back foot and turn to the front, with left leg outstretched (2) (3)
- Bring your left leg across your right, with both knees bent (4)
- Step to the left (5)
- Bring your left knee over your right (remembering to use those hips) (6)
- Step to the right (7)
- Turn to your left, with left foot behind the right in mirror image of start (8)
- Repeat in the opposite direction

SCD
42

1 2 3

4 5

- Start with feet hip distance apart and weight on the right foot (1)
- Go up onto the balls of your feet and bring your left leg across your right, twisting at the waist (2)
- Bring your left leg back to the side (3)
- Then tap behind with the left leg, remaining on your toes (4)
- Bring leg back to side and tap in front again (5)

  Do in sets of eight on each side, starting with one set and working up to three.
  Make sure you are using your arms and twisting at the waist throughout

CHA CHA CHA

Move 6
Cha Cha Box

1   2   3   4   5

As opposite only with a turn.

- Start as opposite (Cha Cha Twist), (arms outstretched in right angle if preferred)
- Step left foot over right, as in the twist (1)
- Return left foot to the side and tap behind (2)
- Bring leg back to side and tap in front (3)
- Tap right leg out to the side and turn 90 degrees to the left (4)
- Repeat on four sides of 'the box' (5) until you turn back to the original position

Move 7
Cha Cha Hip Roll

1   2   3

- Stand with feet hip distance apart and arms stretched above head (1)
- Move your hips to the left side (2)
- With a circular movement roll your hips to the right (3)
- Return to centre and continue
- Repeat eight times each way

Car dealer turned TV star Dominic Littlewood is out to settle old scores on *Strictly Come Dancing*. As a guest on the BBC2 game show *Sudo-Q*, he knocked Len Goodman out of play, before losing to Anton du Beke. The presenter of *Don't Get Done, Get Dom* decided he wouldn't get mad, he'd get even – by beating Anton at his own game. But he is still hoping Len isn't holding any grudges!

minic Littlewood

Dom's route to television fame has not been a conventional one. He was selling new and used cars in Essex when his cheeky and charismatic personality caught the attention of producers from Channel 4's *Faking It*. In 2001 he made his TV debut on the show, teaching a vicar to be a second-hand car dealer in just one month. His memorable appearance on the show landed him a co-presenting job on BBC2's *Wrong Car, Right Car*, and he went on to front the BBC's *To Buy or Not to Buy*, *How I Made My Property Fortune* and *Beat the Burglar*. More recently, he helped members of the public get good deals in *Don't Get Done, Get Dom*, and he is currently a reporter on *The One Show*.

The 42-year-old Essex boy has no previous dance experience, apart from the odd night out. 'After a couple of drinks, I start thinking I can dance,' he says. 'But I end up embarrassing myself because I have two left feet – and they're both on backwards!'

Nonetheless, he hopes to fall in love with dancing during the course of the show. 'I don't want to be the first to go out because I really want to learn lots about dancing,' he says. 'I hope I end up enjoying dancing so much that I'll carry on afterwards – that would nearly be as good as winning. But I'm extremely competitive, so I'd love to win. I believe if you can't win, cheat!'

Given the choice between Latin and ballroom, the popular presenter admits he doesn't think he'll be great at either. As a rock 'n' roll fan, his favourite dance is the Jive and he's excited about learning the moves. 'I've loved rock 'n' roll music since I was a kid,' he says. 'And I always wished that I could learn how to do the Jive.'

A qualified scuba diver, Dom is super-fit and has a passion for water sports, including water-skiing barefoot, sailing and jet skiing. But he reveals that, thanks to an accident in his youth, he is lucky he can walk – let alone dance! 'When I was 25, I broke my neck in Australia', he explains. 'I'd been out sailing and was showing off to some girls on the beach. My mate was a big lad – a rugby player – and he picked me up, tossed me in the air and I came down on my head.'

Dom snapped a vertebra in his neck and nearly severed his spinal chord. He was in hospital for a month and lucky not to have died or been paralysed. 'Thankfully, the injury hasn't given me any problems since, and I sometimes think it's stronger now than it was before!'

'I'm extremely competitive, so I'd love to win. I believe if you can't win, cheat!'

The Story of Series Two
The Good, the Bad and Quentin Willson

1 Sarah's ladylike Manners

For series two, the celebrities had the advantage of knowing what they were letting themselves in for this time, but there were shocks in store for some of the dancers. Brendan's partner, *Casualty* star Sarah Manners, was something of a ladette who demonstrated her skill at burping, ate garlic, came to training with a hangover and then played air guitar on the floor. 'She's definitely the exception to the rule of the perfect partner,' sniffed Brendan in despair.

2 Who, me?

Veteran TV presenter Esther Rantzen came to the show describing herself as 'a little old lady with a hump' but she was soon in the capable hands of Anton du Beke. 'I am the greatest dancer in the world,' declared the hoofer. After their charming Waltz to 'Moon River', Esther couldn't believe her ears when Arlene told her, 'You danced like a true professional.' Sadly, it was all downhill from there.

3 Quentin sets a new low

Hazel gained the judges' sympathy when she got lumbered with rhythmically challenged former *Top Gear* presenter Quentin Willson. Even Quentin's son, Max, reacted in horror at what he saw: 'Daddy's dancing is not very good.' Sure enough, their Cha Cha Cha was a pile-up. The couple were awarded eight points, before crashing out in the first round.

4 Jill's a scarlet woman

Jill Halfpenny opened the second show with a raunchy Rumba to 'Lady in Red', and set the tone for the rest of the series. The judges' score of 32 put Jill and Darren top of the leader board, where they were destined to stay for the next five weeks.

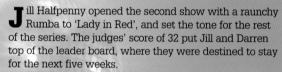

5 Diarmuid and disaster

After the judges said he lacked the talent to dance, Diarmuid became the first celebrity to reduce a dancer to tears with his attempts. 'I don't really know how to work with him,' sobbed his poor partner Nicole. The couple's Quickstep left the judges cold. 'The Quickstep is like a soufflé. It's light and fluffy,' lamented Len. 'This was more like a spotted dick.'

6 Paul's plank of pain!

Carol Vorderman may be good with figures but the judges thought her week-one Waltz was 'stiff' and her friends christened her the 'dancing dalek'. In week two, Paul employed a novel way to loosen her up – if she didn't wiggle enough, he smacked her bottom with a plank! Sadly, it couldn't save the couple, and they were voted off.

Roger and Camilla

Sarah and Brendan

Julian and Erin

Jill and Darren

Diarmuid and Nicole

Esther and Anton

7 Dance, little sister

As he started on the show, Julian declared that he was looking forward to dancing with a woman. 'I haven't done that since 1973,' he said. But footwork wasn't his forte, and after week one's Cha Cha Cha, he was described as 'just dreadful' by Craig, Julian looked to his sister Frankie, an ex-dancer, for support. With her help, he soon proved that the Quickstep was more his style.

8 Roger's Travolta tribute

Roger and Camilla borrowed from Quentin – Tarantino rather than Willson – for their *Pulp Fiction*-style Jive. To the classic Chuck Berry track, 'You Never Can Tell', Roger mimicked the John Travolta moves perfectly, but the panel's opinion was split. Len and Arlene loved it, but for Craig it was 'far too heavy', while Bruno said it was 'clumsy'.

9 Waite 'til I get you home

Ian Waite and Denise Lewis were getting on so well, he decided to take her home to meet his mum. Dance instructor Mary's advice to strive for 'more energy levels', led Ian to Jive so enthusiastically he ripped the seat of his trousers. Poor Denise also bruised the balls of her feet so badly she could hardly walk. On the night, she battled through to receive a slightly disappointing 25.

10 Aled's thumb injury

Denise wasn't the only one suffering. Singer Aled Jones aggravated a previous thumb injury during tough training with partner Lilia Kopylova, and it turned a nasty shade of blue. After applying some ice and resting for a while, Aled was back on the floor and delivering a fabulous Jive which earned the couple a very respectable 32.

11 Brendan's apology

After Brendan's Rumba with Sarah was savaged by the judges, he refused to talk to his partner after the show. The training for week three began with Sarah in tears but she did manage to achieve an apology from the great man – albeit in the third person. 'Brendan said something he shouldn't have said,' admitted the sheepish dancer. 'It was said in haste and I'm very, very sorry.' All harmony restored, the pair managed a tension-filled Tango which Len described as 'fabulous, fabulous, fabulous'.

12 Esther's cruise control

Esther was booked to speak on a cruise ship in the Caribbean in week three, so Anton was forced to join her. As they practised the Tango on deck, fellow passenger Heather was on hand with a bit of guidance. 'Put your knee between his legs,' she advised. 'You've got to forget your modesty and get in there!' Esther, unfortunately, went overboard (not literally, of course) with fishnet stockings and a garter. Craig called the routine 'an absolute disaster', and Anton and Esther walked the plank.

Aled and Lilia

Denise and Ian

Carol and Paul

Quentin and Hazel

The Story of Series Two Continued

13 · Roger gets man-to-man training

Week four saw some fancy tactical footwork on the part of the dancers, with Paul Killick drafted in to help Julian, and Anton partnering Roger to help him with his lack of confidence. 'Just imagine you are me!' was Anton's top tip. In the live show Arlene gasped, 'A beautiful Foxtrot. Boy, did you work those size 13s!'

14 · Dominant Diarmuid's last stand

A despondent Diarmuid admitted he was fed up with being 'bottom of the class', but at the end of the week his steps improved and on the night, Len dubbed him 'dominant Diarmuid'. Even Craig displayed his softer side – well, sort of. 'I know how hard it is learning to dance and I know it takes great courage,' he said. 'But you possess absolutely no dance talent whatsoever.' With a score of 17, his highest of the series, it was time for the game gardener to go back to his potting shed.

15 · Double trouble

Jill couldn't believe her eyes when Darren's twin brother popped in during training. Dale, who is also a dance teacher, had flown in from America to lend his support. 'There are two of them!' screamed Jill.

16 · Blackpool rocks

As the competition hotted up, the six remaining couples headed to Blackpool for week five. The fabulous Tower Ballroom is the spiritual home of ballroom dancing and the contestants performed an elegant Viennese Waltz to rapturous applause. Afterwards, the judges picked their favourites, with Craig going for Jill and Darren, and the other three plumping for Denise and Ian.

17 · Ian pumps iron

After Ian had admonished Denise for a lack of improvement the previous week, Denise turned the tables and, accusing her tutor of being 'a little bit unfit', dragged him to the gym for a gruelling workout.

18 · What's so funny?

On Arlene's advice, Ian enrolled Denise in some ballet lessons to improve the look of her hands and feet, but when Ian turned up in his leg warmers, Denise couldn't dance for laughing! On the night, however, she did stop giggling long enough to pull off a triumphant Tango and a pouting Paso Doble. With a combined score of 71 out of 80, Denise and Ian finished on top of the leader board for the first time in five weeks.

19 — Jives and jibes

Ever since Julian referred to Craig as 'the ugly one on the end' at the beginning of the series, the insults had been flying. After a less than perfect Jive, Craig commented that 'the jacket and the shoes did all the work', to which Julian replied, 'You've got too much foundation on!' Not to be beaten, Craig shot back 'That won't change the fact that that Jive was terrible.'

20 — Aled's final fling

He started the series saying, 'I'm hoping for a massive power cut on Saturday night,' but by the semi-final Aled Jones had lost weight, toned up and had actually learned to dance. His first dance brought high praise from Len and Bruno. Unfortunately, the choice of music – the *Chicago* show tune 'He Had it Coming' – proved prophetic and Aled and Lilia were out.

21 — Halfpenny is the full shilling

In the final, Jill and Darren earned 34 points with their fabulous Foxtrot but were still behind Denise and Ian by four (precious) points. Then came the Jive to the appropriate number 'I'm Still Standing' – and the judges were blown away. They showed their appreciation by awarding the couple the first ever score of 40 out of 40.

22 — Julian's an officer, not a gentleman

For the first dance of the final Julian went all Richard Gere in a white naval uniform, sweeping Erin into his arms like a conquering hero. But the competition was fierce and the only conquering he was doing was of his own nerves. The Quickstep led to another

sniping match when Craig called it 'substandard'. Julian, in anything but gentlemanly terms, called the judge a 'silly old queen'.

23 — Denise goes for gold

Denise promised that she and Ian would 'explode on to the dance floor' on the final show and they did just that. Their score of 38 put them in the lead but a slippery floor in the Samba lost them a couple of crucial points and meant that the Olympic gold medallist had to settle for silver.

24 — Jill's trophy moment

After eight weeks of hard work and aching muscles, *EastEnders* star Jill Halfpenny was named as the second winner of *Strictly Come Dancing*. 'It's amazing!' she gasped, and she had a few words for her dance partner too. 'Darren, you're a brilliant teacher,' she told him. 'I've really enjoyed this experience and that has a lot to do with you. Thank you very much.'

Series Two
Winner's Story
Jill Halfpenny

Jill Halfpenny's journey from Albert Square to the Blackpool Tower was a delight to watch. From day one the Newcastle-born actress threw herself enthusiastically into the spirit of the show and hardly put a foot wrong. Although she hadn't danced since learning ballet and tap as a child, it all came flooding back as soon as she started rehearsing with dance partner Darren Bennett. 'It definitely helped,' she says. 'Some people started out having to learn how to hear the rhythm in the music but to me that came naturally.'

Jill, who starred as Phil Mitchell's girlfriend, Kate, in *EastEnders*, was thrilled to be partnered with hard-working Darren Bennett and was determined to give it her all from the very start. 'Darren is very strict and very precise,' says Jill. 'And he's a perfectionist, which suits me fine, because I am too. We had a lot of fun together but we have the same ethos. We both wanted to work hard and put 100 per cent into it.'

Working four to five hours a day can be tough on the muscles but even tougher on the ladies' feet, as Jill was to discover. 'As soon as you start rehearsing, you are dancing in high heels!' laughs Jill. 'It is very strange to begin with but after a while you forget about the blisters and stop thinking about it. At the start my feet were so sore I could hardly walk but by week three they were as hard as nails!'

Jill and Darren's Waltz was scheduled last on the opening show of the series and, at the time, Jill said the wait made her 'sick to my stomach'. The judges spotted her promise immediately, with Len declaring, 'I can see tremendous potential here. Fabulous, well done.'

Jill and Darren went from strength to strength and by show six they had been top of the leader board on five consecutive shows, and had prompted one of Bruce's brilliant gags. 'Last week Jill's dancing was so exciting judge Len nearly had a stroke,' he quipped. 'Thank goodness he wasn't near enough to reach her!' By the semi-final, though, the judges were getting picky and Jill's Tango proved a slight blot on her copybook. 'Jill wasn't in control,' griped Arlene. 'And you have to start using your upper spine.'

By the night of the final, the slow Foxtrot received a mixed reaction from the judges and a score of 34, but the Jive, once again, blew them away. The couple made history with the first perfect score of 40 out of 40 ever awarded on the show. Craig called the dance 'phenomenal', while Bruno yelled, 'An explosion of talent!' Len declared it 'the best dance of the whole series' and

The couple made history with the first perfect score of 40 out of 40 ever awarded on the show

Arlene paid Jill the highest compliment she could by saying, 'As a choreographer, I bow to you, Jill. Sensational. Dazzling. I hope that one day I get to work with you.' Finishing with a high score of 74, the judges' favourite was backed up by the public and Jill and Darren romped home to win the trophy.

Jill's mum was first to congratulate her – running on to the stage to give her daughter an ecstatic hug, only to be shepherded off by Bruce, who had no idea who she was! 'My mum was so proud,' laughs Jill. 'It was a brilliant moment.'

Jill's partner at home, Craig Conway, was not only thrilled that she had won but, no doubt, slightly relieved it was over! 'He was over the moon,' says Jill. 'He'd lived and breathed my training. I'd come home every night saying, "I can't do this move" or "We're doing this dance on Saturday", so he lived every moment.' Just as well, as he had a little fancy footwork of his own to do in February 2007, when the acting couple got married. Darren and Lilia choreographed the first dance! After winning series two, Jill's dancing feet took her straight to the West End for a stint in *Chicago*, playing sassy murderess Roxie Hart. '*Strictly* helped in the sense that I was toned up and match fit for all the rehearsing to come,' she says. Now back in television roles, such as *Blue Murder*, Jill is looking forward to Saturday nights in front of the telly. 'I'll definitely be watching the next series,' she says. 'I'm a big fan and I'm looking forward to it.'

Jill on ...

Favourite Dance
I enjoyed a lot of them but obviously my favourite was the Jive and then the Cha Cha Cha. I definitely preferred the Latin to the Ballroom.

Worst Dance
I found the Waltz the most difficult. It's not technically the hardest but it's the one I struggled with. Then again, it was my first week so I'd have liked to have tried it again once I'd improved.

Getting a Perfect Score
Getting the perfect score was fantastic. The audience are always great but the atmosphere in Blackpool, where the final is held, was incredible and the audience went wild when we got the judges' scores.

Facing the Judges
It is terrifying, especially when you feel you could have done better. But I don't mind the criticism. I'm used to that because of the industry I'm in. You take it on the chin and work on it and it's all part of the show.

How Strictly Come Dancing Has Changed Her Life
It changed my profile. I became Jill Halfpenny rather than whichever character I was playing at the time. What struck me was the cross section of people who watched *Strictly*. They included very upper-class people I'd meet at charity dos to families in the supermarket. It's extraordinary.

'I'm used to criticism in my working environment, so I hope I will take it on the chin. I'd hate to start blubbing live on air!'

Kate Garraway's favourite song is 'I Will Survive' and she's hoping that's what she'll do in *Strictly Come Dancing*. The *GMTV* presenter has been a fan of the show since the first series, and to be a contestant herself is a fairy tale come true. 'I'm excited to be taking part because I have always wanted to learn to dance, and I can't wait to dress up like a princess and be whirled around a room by my Prince Charming!'

Kate Garraway

Kate's career in journalism began on BBC Radio and in 1994 she moved to ITV to train as a television reporter. A two-year stint at Sky News followed, before she landed her seat on the *GMTV* sofa in September 2000. The 39-year-old, who is married to fellow journalist Derek Draper and has a baby daughter, Darcey, remembers going to 'Mrs Bubbington's' dance class when she was three or four years old but, apart from the occasional bop at a wedding, has had little dancing experience since. And if her experience in the class is anything to go by, it's not surprising she didn't take it up as a career!

'When I was four, the dancers in the class put on a show,' she explains. 'We had worked for six weeks on a performance and when the curtains opened, myself and a friend completely forgot what we were meant to be doing and stood there talking and pointing out our parents in the audience, while everyone else danced around us.'

Hopefully, history won't repeat itself when Kate graces the dance floor on the live Saturday shows, as her greatest fear is making a complete fool of herself. 'I'm not worried about going out first,' she comments. 'I just want to have a good time. I don't expect to win because I'm much more realistic than that, but I'll give it my best and try my hardest. Hopefully, I'll come away with the ability not to show my family up at weddings.'

Although she is an *SCD* fan, the talented journalist says she doesn't yet know the difference between Latin and ballroom, so she is looking forward to trying both. 'I've always fancied giving the Tango a go but I think it may also be one of the hardest dances,' she says. 'I like the look of it because it is pulsating, passionate and exciting.'

She's obviously not too confident about her style, as she's expecting the worst from the judges. 'If I get any criticism on the show, I'm sure it will be highly justified,' she laughs. 'I'm used to criticism in my working environment, so I hope I will take it on the chin. I'd hate to start blubbing live on air!'

She will be dancing with Anton du Beke

Let's Party!

Diehard dancing fans will be familiar with the frequent Saturday night dilemma – go out and party or stay in and watch *Strictly Come Dancing*. But now you can do both! Throw a *Strictly Come Dancing* party and make your Saturday night as glitzy as the show! All you need is a group of friends – whether it's eight or 80 – and a little (or lots of) glamour.

Geoffrey and
Josephine Bellamy-Smythe

Request the pleasure of your company at an exclusive event to celebrate the final of

Strictly Come Dancing

Drinks and canapés will be served from 6 pm.

Dress: Black tie and ballroom.

RSVP

Theme

Choose the date of your party according to the show you want to share with friends. The final is a favourite but the first week also has plenty of potential when it comes to bets and friendly rivalry.

Make an official handwritten invitation, preferably on white card with gold lettering.

Décor

Unless you live in a stately home, your house may need a little jazzing up for the occasion. Think glitz, glamour and lots of sparkle and you can't go far wrong.

- Raid the discount stores for cheap objects such as candlesticks, gold or silver bowls and sparkly gift ribbon. If you're lucky, you might be able to pick up a gold or silver fringed hanging for a door or wall – perfect for a ballroom look.

- Foil wrapping paper comes in lots of wonderful colours, such as pink, purple or gold, and can be used to cover small tables to add shimmer.

- Alternatively, to give your house more of a tea dance ambience, you could choose fabric tablecloths in a deep rich colour, such as burgundy or red, and cover with a smaller lace cloth. Paper tablecloths in all colours can be bought very cheaply on the internet or at party stores.

- Silver foil platters are best for food and can be complemented with silver or red foil plates, available in party shops and on the internet.

- Add a glitter ball. They can be bought for less that £20 but if you are working on a budget try covering a beach ball in silver foil. Then tie a thread around the air valve and suspend it from the ceiling using a hook or a drawing pin. The ball will spin with the slightest air movement.

- If you really want to make this a party to remember, check out the dance teachers in your area and find out if you can book a home lesson for your guests. It won't come cheap but, if you feel like splashing out, it's a great way to entertain guests and have fun on the dance floor.

Games

Strictly Come Dancing will provide enough entertainment for your guests but, to add to your enjoyment, here are a few suggestions:

- Have a sweepstake at the beginning of the evening. If it's week one, put the names of the celebrities in a hat and let each guest pick one out. Whoever chooses the celebrity knocked out that night, wins.

- If it is the final week you could get your guests to predict the scores for all three couples. When each score is announced, players must score the difference between their prediction and the actual figure (e.g. prediction 36, judges' score 32, player scores 4). The person with the lowest score at the end of the night wins.

- Split into teams of three, one for each celebrity. You can either choose favourite celebrities or pick the names out of a hat. Each team cheers on their chosen celebrity and the winning team gets small prizes. You can extend the idea by having mini-bets along the way, such as bets on who will be the first dancer to get a ten, who will be first out, dress colours etc. Each correct prediction scores points and the team with the highest points gets a prize

- Make some judges' baons out of cardboard with the scores one to ten (two on each bat, on reverse sides). As the couples dance, hold up your own scores and see if they coincide with those of your favourite judge.

Let's Party!

Food

How about providing a *Strictly Come Dancing* theme to your food?
The following are suggestions but you might also have fun thinking up a few yourself.

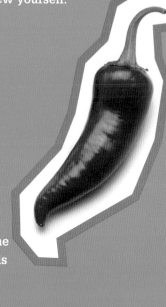

- 'Tango' tortillas with Salsa dip
- Cheese twirls
- Potato twists
- Cha Cha Cha Chilli
- Paso Doble Paella
- Argentinian Choriza
- Teacakes (for the ballroom lovers)
- Viennese Swirl biscuits

Cocktails

As well as the obligatory bubbly, why not liven the
party up with one or two dance-themed cocktails
from the list below.

Rumba

- 1–2 tablespoons (¾ fl oz) Irish Cream (e.g. Baileys)
- 1–2 tablespoons (¾ fl oz) dark rum
- 150 ml (¼ pint) hot black coffee
- 1 teaspoon sugar, or to taste
- 1 tablespoon (½ fl oz) whipping cream

Pour the Irish Cream, rum and coffee
into an Irish coffee cup and sweeten to
taste. Gently float the whipping cream on top and serve.

Foxtrot

- 2–3 tablespoons (1 – 1½ fl oz) rum
- 1 tablespoon (½ fl oz) lemon juice
- 2–3 dashes of orange liqueur (e.g. Cointreau, Grand Marnier etc)
- crushed ice

Put all the ingredients into a cocktail shaker and shake with the ice.
Then strain into a chilled cocktail glass, and serve.

Cream Samba

- 1 tablespoon (½ fl oz) brandy
- 3 tablespoons (1¼ fl oz) coconut liqueur
- 65 g (2½ oz) ice cream
- crushed ice
- desiccated coconut or fruit, to garnish

Place all the ingredients into a blender with some crushed ice. Blend for two minutes. Pour into a cocktail glass and garnish with desiccated coconut or fruit.

Southern Tango

- 2 tablespoons (1 fl oz) dry vermouth
- 1 tablespoon (½ fl oz) peach liqueur
- 4 tablespoons (2 fl oz) lemonade
- crushed ice
- a twist of lemon peel

Pour all the ingredients into a highball glass or tall tumbler three-quarters filled with crushed ice. Add a twist of lemon peel, and serve.

Italian Delight – one for Bruno!

- 2 tablespoons (1 fl oz) amaretto
- 3 tablespoons (1½ oz) single cream
- crushed ice
- 1 cherry

In a cocktail shaker, shake all the ingredients, except the cherry, with the ice and strain into a chilled cocktail glass. Add the cherry on top and serve.

Strawberry Daquiri – as Cuban as the Rumba

- 3 tablespoons (1½ fl oz) rum
- 1 tablespoon (½ fl oz) strawberry liqueur
- 3-4 strawberries (depending on their size)
- 3-4 tablespoons (1½– 2 fl oz) lemon juice
- a cup of crushed ice

Mix all the ingredients in a blender until you have a thick consistency. Serve in a cocktail glass.

Ballroom Dancer Cake

This cake is relatively simple to make and looks incredibly impressive. The top half of a child's doll is visible and the decorated cake forms her beautiful ball gown skirt. You can make it with any sponge recipe (e.g. chocolate) but here is the classic Victoria sponge version. You'll need a Barbie™-type doll or a craft doll (sold in some craft shops) and a metal or pyrex pudding bowl (2.25 litre/4 pints capacity).

- 125 g (4 oz) butter
- 125 g (4 oz) caster sugar
- 2 eggs, beaten
- 25 g (4 oz) self-raising flour
- vanilla essence or 1 teaspoon grated lemon rind

For the icing:

- 150g (5 oz) butter, softened
- 300 g (10 oz) icing sugar
- 1-2 tablespoons milk
- a few drops of food colouring
- cake decorations of your choice

Preheat the oven to 190°C/375°F/Gas Mark 5. For the cake 'skirt', put the butter and sugar in a mixing bowl or food mixer, and whisk until light and creamy. Slowly add the beaten eggs and a little of the flour. Fold in the remaining flour and add the flavouring. Pour the mixture into a metal pudding bowl and bake for 20-25 minutes or until a skewer inserted into the cake comes out clean. Cool for 15 minutes and turn out on to a wire rack.

For the icing, beat the butter until soft. Add half the icing sugar and beat until smooth. Add the remaining icing sugar with one tablespoon of the milk. Beat until creamy, then add the food colouring and mix well. If the consistency is too runny, add a little extra icing sugar.

When the cake is cool, insert your doll up to its waist, then decorate it with icing and cake decorations. If the top half of your doll is not clothed, use icing to make the top of the dress as well.

The *Fearsome* Foursome

Bruno Tonioli is the peacock of judges – flamboyant, colourful and very noisy! His trademark metaphors and florid language are guaranteed to raise a smile and, if he sees a dance he likes, he is always effusive in his praise. The passionate Italian has compared dancers to 'an Emperor penguin with an egg between its legs', 'Godzilla or a praying mantis' and 'the perfect Tiramisu'. But with thirty years in the business, as both dancer and choreographer, he knows exactly what he's talking about.

'I ran away from home at 18 and got my first job as the lead in a French dance company,' he reveals. 'I was discovered, really, because one of the guys who played the lead walked out and I got my break. I left home, left my mother, packed my bag and went to Paris, and I never went back.'

Growing up in Italy, Bruno was not encouraged to indulge his passion for dance and was steered towards a more academic route. But the fiery nature that viewers see on *Strictly Come Dancing* shone through and his determination took over. 'I had to do everything without telling my parents,' he recalls. 'It was a nightmare. It was very hard for me. They wanted me to go to school and university, but I used to sneak out for singing and dancing lessons without telling them. When you want something so much your life depends on it you just do it. I knew if I didn't I would probably end up in a ditch somewhere. I was so determined and I fought so hard – I don't know if I could ever do it again!'

Despite his parents' objections, Bruno went on to become a successful dancer, touring Europe in his first company, before joining a London dance troupe. He starred in pop videos, including Elton John's 'I'm Still Standing', before becoming a choreographer and working with such stars as Tina Turner, Mick Jagger, Michael Jackson and Paul McCartney. He has also worked on numerous films, including *Little Voice* with Jane Horrocks and Michael Caine, and *Enigma* with Kate Winslet.

His success meant he was able to build bridges with his parents before they sadly passed away.

Bruno

'My mother was devastated when I left,' says Bruno. 'She turned around eventually but it took a few years. Both my parents are dead now but fortunately they saw my career going very well before they died. They saw me become a successful choreographer and all the worry evaporated – but it took a good ten years.'

By coincidence, one of the jobs Bruno took on as a young dancer was Bruce Forsyth's television show – for which he did an impression of Rod Stewart –

and he is delighted to be working with Bruce again. 'I hadn't seen him since I did the show and he hasn't changed,' marvels the jubilant judge. 'He's exactly the same! Is he pickled or something? And the energy the man's got! He's 80 next year and he's incredible.'

After the runaway success of the last four series, Bruno is looking forward to starting series five and is delighted the show brings pleasure to so many. 'It's like a Christmas tree of a show,' he says. 'You switch it on and it makes you happy. It's fun, it's glamorous and it's one of the shows that everybody seems to enjoy. It's wonderful, especially in the winter when the days are short and you put on this show and everybody has a grin on their faces. It is pure Saturday night!'

No doubt, series five will see the usual spats between the four judges but, Bruno reveals, the fighting ends when the cameras stop rolling. 'We get it out of the way while we are on,' he laughs. 'Once it's done, it's done. You can't carry it with you and if we all said the same thing, how boring would that be?' He adds, 'Craig is

> 'If we all said the same thing, how boring would that be?'

such a bitch on the programme but off-screen he's much nicer. Of all of us, he is the one who changes the most. He is very laid-back and Australian – give him a drink and he's happy!'

As a *Blue Peter* presenter, Gethin Jones is no stranger to a challenge. He has flown with the Red Arrows, been attacked by an alligator and fought as a Samurai Warrior in Japan – but can he tackle the Tango? 'I agreed to take part for the very same reasons as I joined *Blue Peter*,' he says. 'I especially enjoy having a go at something I don't think I'm very good at.' There was also a bit of family pressure as Gethin's big sister, Mererid, is a massive *Strictly* fan and she would never forgive him if he didn't take part because she loves the show so much!

Gethin Jones

Born in Cardiff, Gethin started presenting on Welsh channel S4C, where he fronted *Popty*, the Welsh equivalent of *Top of the Pops*. From there, he took on a live youth magazine show called *UNED 5* for two and a half years, before landing the sought after job at *Blue Peter*. As well as presenting *Jones, Jones, Jones* at Cardiff's Millennium Centre – where the world record was broken for the biggest gathering of people with the same surname – he is the envy of many a sci-fi fan after appearing as a Cyberman in a recent episode of *Doctor Who*.

The six-foot Welshman looks like he could cut quite a dash on the dance floor and says that when he was younger, he really wanted to be Shakin' Stevens! And he admits that he took up folk dancing at secondary school – for the love of a woman.

He will be dancing with *Camilla Dallerup*

'I decided to join the group because I fancied a girl who was a member,' he says. 'I danced with the group for three whole years before I got to be her dancing partner, and then it was only for five and a half minutes on the stage at the National Eisteddfod! It was worth the wait, though, as she gave me a kiss on the cheek afterwards.'

One thing the children's favourite does have is rhythm, which should stand him in good stead. He fondly remembers a trip to Madagascar, for *Blue Peter*, where he attended a concert. 'When the music started playing, I just had to dance,' he recalls. 'The locals thought that I was part of the concert and started to surround me, clapping enthusiastically.' The production crew fell about laughing but Gethin carried on, thinking the applause meant he was a bit of a legendary dancer!

A newcomer to ballroom and Latin, Gethin is yet to discover which he prefers, but he is looking forward to the Jive. And, as he is the first civilian to have completed the gruelling Royal Marine Commando 30-mile yomp, the training should be a doddle. Even so, he knows he has a lot to live up to. 'I have no dancing background whatsoever, and it never ceases to amaze me the standards the celebrity novices achieve every Saturday night,' he says.

And, while he's out to win, he will settle with wowing the audience once or twice along the way. 'Maybe a movement that gets me a spontaneous round of applause,' he comments, 'that would be a great achievement for me.'

'I have no dancing background whatsoever, and it never ceases to amaze me the standards the celebrity novices achieve every Saturday night'

Strictly Stunning

Stylist Su Judd has been behind the show's fabulous frocks and sassy suits since series one. She chooses her favourite outfits from the first four series and tells the story behind each one.

Karen's Pink and Black Viennese Waltz Dress

Karen knows what she likes and she came in to see me saying she wanted a really big dress for her Viennese Waltz with Mark Ramprakash in series four. She had done her research and brought in some pictures of lovely wedding dresses, so we came up with this fantastic swirling skirt and beautiful black beading on the corset. Arlene was really taken with it and said, 'You look like a Christian Dior model on the catwalk in the 1950s.' That was great because no one ever mentions the outfits! After the show lots of people wrote in wanting to buy the dress and, in the end, it was auctioned off to the public.

Clare King's Silver Foxtrot Dress

Clare had been sexy and hot all the way through series four, so for the ballroom dance she wanted something classy. This elegant, silver ball gown was based on a Chanel swimsuit. I took a picture of the neckline and designed it around that. She had a floating piece of silver chiffon which was held on to her arms with flesh-coloured straps to stop it falling off as she whirled around the dance floor. She looked lovely.

Denise Lewis's Lime Green Bikini Samba Dress

Denise was fantastic to work with during series two and I loved this outfit because no one else could have got away with that colour and style. She was a treat for us because she was used to being seen in athletics gear and she loved dressing up and looking feminine. She has very broad shoulders and she's quite muscular, so we chose outfits that would tone the shoulders down and make her look slimmer – but she was up for it all!

Emma Bunton's Orange and Black Samba Dress

This is the basic *Moulin Rouge* look which we use a lot in the costumes. The corsets are very flattering and you can sculpt any figure out of it. As we had a few problems with Emma's designs, we literally constructed the black and orange dress on her. Then we stuck all kinds of bits on her to make the ruffle effect at the back.

Camilla's Trick Rumba Dress

Camilla's dress for the Rumba with Roger Black in series two was a simple black number that turned into a red dress when some material cascaded down from the chest. It's a good trick to employ if your partner can't dance, as it distracts attention away from him. Actually, it's an old trick of Ian Waite's which Camilla suggested we try for the programme. The red material was rolled inside a flap which she pulled down halfway through the routine. The leotard she was wearing had been on both Lilia and Carol but we redesigned it and put feathers on the tail, then added the trick material.

Carol Smillie's Jade Green Salsa Dress

This sexy outfit created for series four consisted of a Lycra bra and skirt with long fringes in a deep sea green, with black bondage straps at the waist. It was very racy. The week after she wore it Carol said, 'My husband was particularly impressed with the dress. He wants me to take it home!'

Strictly
Stunning

Out of numerous celebrities Su has worked with, and the hundreds of outfits that she has designed, some are more memorable than others – and not always for the right reasons.

Gloria Hunniford's White Waltz Dress

For the first show people are terrified and the dress suddenly becomes a big deal because the outfits are key to the way they feel and perform on the night. During series three, Gloria felt like the older statesman on the show and was very conscious of her age. There was added pressure because her partner, Darren, had won the year before, with Jill Halfpenny, and she was very keen not to look a frump. I went down to Gloria's house to tweak a few things and she was very nervous, but she is such a lovely lady and so nice to everyone.

Sarah Manners and Brendan's Paso Doble Outfits

All male dancers are very controlling. Even Darren, who has the sweetest temperament, knows what he wants, because the dresses have to complement their outfits and make them look good. For the Paso Doble with Sarah Manners, we had designed a turquoise and gold Egyptian style outfit but, at the last minute, the routine was changed to a more Gothic dance and the outfit had to change too. I had a costume that had been made for Lilia so I put that on Sarah. She is a significantly different shape so we cut it in half and built another section into the middle, then we created the skirt from scraps of purple material.

Matt Dawson's Pink Shirt

I really do regret putting Matt Dawson in the pink shirt in the first show of series four. When the celebrities first come to the show, I do a consultation with them and we design the outfits accordingly. Matt was so accommodating and open to ideas, that I got a bit carried away and made the most mental shirt! The first shirt a dancer wears creates an instant impression, but I think this one was a bit over the top.

Lilia's Disappearing Samba Dress

Lilia's Samba dress in series three was the biggest wardrobe disaster we've ever had. The stylists and designers are usually watching with bated breath, hoping that nothing will go wrong, and this time it did. The whole dress fell apart! We had designed the dress to make Lilia look as naked as possible, and it had traps and clips all over it to keep it in place. One of the clips wasn't locked properly and it came apart. She had to do the whole dance with one hand across her chest, holding it up. However, she was very professional and good about it afterwards. Luckily, she and Darren got through and won, otherwise she might have been a lot more upset!

'I think *Strictly* will be a good opportunity for people to see another side to me, and I hope they will be surprised. There is more to me than boobs and a smile!'

If anyone can add more glamour to the glitziest show of all, it's Kelly Brook. The Kent-born model, who topped the *FHM* list of the 100 Sexiest Women in the World in 2005, is bound to look fabulous in the skimpy Latin costumes, but she didn't get off on the best foot in the dancing. At the *SCD* titles shoot, she and her dance partner were performing a simple spin and they both ended up on the floor!

Kelly Brook

Nonetheless, Kelly has come a long way from her stage experience as a 15-year-old. 'I was in a pantomime and I played the front end of "Daisy, the cow",' she laughs. 'My friend was the back end and we had to go on stage and dance a jig.'

Although she began modelling at 16, after winning a beauty contest, Kelly has since carved out a career in acting and presenting. Educated at the world-famous Italia Conti stage school in London, she moved into television at just 17, when she fronted youth programmes for Granada Television. Two years later, she was chosen to replace Denise van Outen as the female half of *The Big Breakfast* team, alongside Johnny Vaughan. From there, she went on to present reality television programme *Celebrity Love Island* for ITV.

After her success in Britain, Kelly set out to conquer Hollywood. Within three weeks, she had landed the lead role in *The (Mis) Adventures of Fiona Plum* and was then offered the part of Lex Luthor's girlfriend in *Smallville*. Since then, Kelly has starred in films such as *School for Seduction*, *House of 9* with Dennis Hopper and *Three* and *Fishtales*, both with fiancé Billy Zane. In the meantime, she has also found time to design a range of swimwear for New Look and is about to launch a book and a new perfume.

Although she is one of the best known models in the UK, Kelly feels that *Strictly Come Dancing* will reveal another side to her. 'I won't mind the criticism because I have always been criticised,' she says. 'I am such an easy target because I have a bouncy personality and big boobs. I think *Strictly* will be a good opportunity for people to see another side to me, and I hope they will be surprised. There is more to me than boobs and a smile!'

A big fan of the show, she particularly loved the last series and thought Mark Ramprakash was amazing. 'His hips were the best entertainment ever!' she says. 'The final show was the best TV experience; the energy was fabulous and I really wanted to be a part of the magic.'

The 27-year-old star is determined not to let her dance partner down. 'I am hoping to learn some new dance skills but I also really want to win,' she says. More than anything, Kelly wants the audience to be entertained and, if her favourite film is anything to go by, she is bound to succeed. '*Dirty Dancing* is something I grew up with and I have fond memories of watching the journey of someone who couldn't dance learn in such a magical way. I'm hoping to recreate the *Dirty Dancing* story during my *SCD* experience,' she

She will be dancing with Brendan Cole

The Fearsome Foursome

Craig Revel Horwood's blunt criticisms have earned him the title of Strictly Come Dancing's Mr Nasty – and made trips to the supermarket somewhat hazardous. 'A couple of old ladies have smashed into my shopping trolley while I've been out shopping,' he laughs. 'They say, "Ooh, you were nasty last night" or "He's my favourite, please be nice to him" but I'm not going to be nice to someone because some old bag in a shopping mall crashes into me and tells me to!'

Craig makes no apology for his opinions. 'The viewers all have their favourites but I can't have one unless they are particularly good dancers, like Emma Bunton, who I thought was fantastic,' he says. 'I was full of praise for her and I got slammed for having favourites, which I think is just crazy. Of course I'm going to have favourites – if people can dance, I'll love them. If they can't, I want them off the show.'

Harsh though his words may be, they are backed up by a wealth of experience in the world of dance. Having taken to dancing after seeing *Grease* and *Saturday Night Fever* in the seventies, Craig left his native Australia to dance at the Lido in Paris before moving to London to try his hand (and his dancing feet) at West End musicals. 'When I first told my parents I wanted to dance, Dad, who was in the navy, thought it was a bit weird that his oldest son was donning a pair of tights and learning dance steps!' reveals Craig. 'But there were five of us and my parents encouraged us to pursue what we wanted. I really loved the sense of freedom I had when I was dancing. It was like a drug that I was addicted to.'

Craig danced in numerous West End productions, including *Cats* and *Crazy For You*, before *Miss Saigon* saw him go from cast member to resident director. A year later he embarked on a career as a choreographer. 'I'd worked with different directors and trained with the most wonderful people.' He was nominated for two Olivier awards for *Spend, Spend, Spend* and *My One and Only*, so he had the perfect credentials to sit in judgement on *Strictly Come Dancing*.

'I think the *Strictly Come Dancing* producers wanted someone with a bit of artistic clout and honest views, because if you are going to judge, it should be from a good base of knowledge.' One of the first comments Craig made in the pilot was to resurface occasionally in the next few series. 'I was watching a video of Natasha and Brendan dancing and the first words I said were "Dull dull, dull!". I thought it was the most boring thing I'd seen! I

Craig

'I didn't realise people thought I was the nasty one until people started booing'

actually thought the programme would get no more than three million viewers and, of course, I was completely wrong.'

Craig's straight-talking style soon earned him a reputation as the harshest of the judges but, he reveals, he never intended to take on that role. 'I didn't realise people thought I was the nasty one until people started booing,' he says. 'I thought that was just my honest opinion! I don't go out of my way to be nasty because I'm actually very encouraging to people who can dance, but people tend to associate me with the negative comments. Sometimes we don't have enough time to express everything we want to say in the ten seconds we have.'

However, his sharp tongue has got him into trouble in the past. After comedienne Jan Ravens was voted off the show, her husband took exception to Craig's less-than-flattering comments. 'Jan was upset and I went up to her in the bar afterwards and said, "Commiserations, darling,"' he explains. 'She said, "Don't talk to me. Just go away!" and her husband started pushing me away and swore a bit at me. It was

'If people can dance, I'll love them. If they can't, I want them off the show'

really embarrassing. You can't just blame one judge for you going out – there are 12 million people voting and the viewers have 50 per cent of the vote. I was just enlightening people as to whether her dance was good or bad, and it happened to be not very good that day.'

Although Craig stands by his artistic criticism, he admits he regrets the one occasion when the banter got a little too personal. 'I did go too far with Patsy Palmer,' he says. 'She said I didn't know what I was talking about and I said, "That's a bit rich coming from someone in a puffer jacket who cries all the time in a two-bit soap!" I do regret saying it because it was personal and I shouldn't get personal.'

While his harsh words may upset the celebrities and dancers, Craig has quite a fan base outside of the studio. 'The public are all thumbs up,' he laughs. 'It's hilarious. They love it. I think because Britain loves a bit of humiliation. That's why they encourage some of the worst dancers to continue in the competition. I guess we're all up for a good laugh at someone else's expense but that's not my job, so it's up to the audience to decide whether they put someone through.'

Craig on …

The Judges

Len is from the ballroom world and as head judge nurtures and encourages the dancers. Bruno is very floral, to say the least, and Arlene can be bitchy as well as fall in love with the pec deck! So we're all very different. If we were all from the ballroom world it would be quite a dull scenario.

On Emma Bunton

I was disappointed that Emma didn't win but Mark was amazing. I think people vote on the journey, the fact that they go from nothing to something extraordinary, and I think that was Mark Ramprakash's story. It was really tough for Emma, because it's a completely different kind of dancing to what she would have done with the Spice Girls – bopping around in a boob tube.

The Worst Dancer

Fiona Phillips! She was dreadful but she has a fantastic personality. I loved her and after the show she was always charming, great fun, and that's what the show is about.

The Best Dancer

Jill Halfpenny was amazing. I had to give her a ten and that's a rare occasion! The runner-up to that, for me, was Colin Jackson. He was phenomenal. He was technically very good but the puppet dance was one of the worst things I've ever seen in my life!

Series Five

John Barnes MBE is swapping football for ballroom to please his growing brood. The former Liverpool player, who has six children, ranging in age from one to 22, says they are delighted he has agreed to take part. 'I've been asked to do a lot of reality TV shows, but my kids have always insisted I would embarrass them,' he says. 'This time, they really wanted me to be a part of the show because they are big fans, so I had to say yes.'

John Barnes

Born in Kingston, Jamaica, John says that music and dancing was always part of his upbringing. 'I grew up in the Caribbean, with people dancing all round me, and so I'm much more used to the looser Latin style of dancing rather than the formal ballroom style.'

John's family moved to the UK when he was a boy and he started playing football for non-league Sudbury Court, where he was spotted by a scout from Watford. After a successful game in Watford's reserves, he was signed in 1981 for the price of a football kit. After taking a leading role in Watford's rise to prominence, he was spotted by England manager Bobby Robson and went on to become England's most capped black player, with 79 caps.

In 1987, John left Watford to join Liverpool, and in his first season at Anfield, the club won the league title. In an 18-year career, John racked up an impressive 752 appearances for four clubs, scoring 562 goals, and in 1997, was awarded an MBE. Since his 1999 retirement, John has worked as head coach for Scottish giants Celtic, and carved out a successful career as a TV pundit, now working as one of Channel 5's principle football presenters. He is also an ambassador for Save the Children.

He will be dancing with Nicole Cutler

As he grew up in a musical family, John is a natural mover and has even provided raps on a couple of hit records: 'Anfield Rap' in 1988 and New Order's 'World in Motion' in 1990. 'I'm not shy when it comes to dancing,' he says. 'I have always danced in nightclubs in the past, but this type of dancing is totally new to me. I just hope I can do the right steps and not look a fool.'

And, of course, he wants to win. 'There's no point being involved in the competition if you don't have a desire to win,' he says. 'I don't want to be knocked out of the competition early. I want to go as far as possible and give a decent performance each week.'

Like his days on the football pitch, the 44-year-old sportsman knows that it doesn't pay to argue with the referee – or judge. 'I always listen to the expert's view,' he says. 'When it comes to dancing, who am I to say what's wrong or right?'

'I have always danced in nightclubs in the past, but this type of dancing is totally new to me'

QUICKSTEP

The Quickstep was introduced in the 1920s, when bands were playing music faster and faster and it proved difficult for dancers to keep up with the traditional Foxtrot. The steps became smaller and quicker and the Charleston, popular throughout Britain and America, was incorporated.

As the name suggest, this is the fastest of the ballroom dances so once you've learned the moves, speed it up – and burn those calories!

Move 1
Pendulum Swings

1

2

- Jumping, swing right leg out to the side (1)
- Bring the right leg down and, without stopping, swing the left leg out (2)
  (The movement resembles that of the classic executive toy,
  a Newton's Cradle)

Move 2
Charleston

1

2

- Put your arms down at your sides with hands turned out and flick your right leg behind you, bending at the knee. **(1)** Keep the left leg slightly bent so you don't lock your knees
- Repeat with the same leg and then flick your left leg **(2)**
- When you have mastered the step, do the Charleston while turning 360 degrees on the spot

Move 3
Quickjumps

1   2   3   4

- Start with feet slightly more than hip distance apart (1)
- Jump in the air, bringing feet together (2)
- Jump again, bringing right leg forward and left leg back in a scissor movement (3)
- Bring feet together and repeat scissor movement, with left leg forward and right behind (4)
- Return to start position
- As you progress, speed these jumps up to double time

Move 4
Side knee dips

1   2

- With hand on hips and knees together, jump slightly forward as you bend your knees on the left-hand diagonal (1)
- Return to centre and dip to the right (2)

Move 5
The Hop

- Bend your left leg and hop on your right leg, while turning 360°
  to your right
- Lead with your right hand (1) (2)
- Repeat in the other direction, hopping on your left leg and leading
  with the left arm (3)

Move 6
Scatter Chasse

- Start with left arm stretched in front and right behind, and step to the left (1)
- Close legs together (2)
- Step to the left again (3)
- Hop onto left leg with right leg raised (4)
- Repeat in the opposite direction

75

Move 7
Jump Squats

1

2

3

- Start with feet together then jump into a squat, pushing your bottom backwards (1)
- Jump back to starting position (2)
- As you progress, turn 90° with each squat (3)

Move 8
The Tiller

1

2

3

- Start with hands on hip and jump with feet together
- Kick your left leg forward (1)
- Jump again and kick your right leg forward (2)
- Jump and kick left leg back (3)
- Repeat with right leg

Len's Lowdown

Head judge Len has ruled the roost since *Strictly Come Dancing* began, watching the inept compete with the elegant. He now reveals what he really thinks of the dancers from the first four series.

Best Five Dances

Jill Halfpenny's Jive

Zoe Ball's Samba

Marl Ramprakash's Tango

Natasha Kaplinsky's slow Foxtrot

Darren Gough's Paso Doble

Worst Performances

Jason Wood's terrible Waltz

Quentin Willson's Cha Cha Cha

Best Couple

The best couple was Jill Halfpenny and Darren Bennett. They were the best ever – in the UK or America – in any series. She is a naturally talented dancer, which is why, after she left *Strictly*, she went straight on to star in the West End production of *Chicago*. She was lovely to watch.

Worst Couple

Again, it would probably be Jason Wood and Kylie Jones because he was so tall. Ballroom dancers need to have a balance, not just in choreography, but in the look of the couple, and they were out of kilter.

Best Improvement

Natasha Kaplinsky, without a doubt – both in her dance performance and her attitude. In the first week, her nerves were in tatters and she was negative about everything. But she got through it and then she started really enjoying herself, and she was eventually the winner!

Most Unfair Eviction

Spoony, definitely, who was out in the third week of series four. That was absolutely ludicrous. I thought he was great, and all the judges did, but the public didn't seem to agree. That was a shock. I think they also got it wrong with Ray Fearon.

Biggest Rule Breaker

Brendan Cole always breaks the most rules. I think he's great on the show, and without him I wouldn't have anyone to get infuriated with!

Surprise Stayer

Julian Clary, who was a great example of someone who kept going longer than he should have done, and Chris Parker in series one. Both made it to the finals. But that's the charm of the show and it's part and parcel of why *Strictly* is so good.

'I would love to do well but, most importantly, I don't want to fall on my backside during the live show!'

Letitia Dean may have to brush off some long-forgotten skills for her turn in *Strictly Come Dancing*. The long-term Albert Square resident, who will celebrate her 40th birthday during the show, hasn't danced since she took ballet, tap and modern at the Sylvia Young Theatre School 24 years ago. 'I sometimes dance around my living room,' she says. 'But the last time I danced in public was at a wedding last year. I have never done any ballroom dancing.'

Letitia Dean

Although she is best known as *EastEnder* Sharon Watts, Letitia was not originally from London but was born in her parents' house in Hatfield, on the grounds of novelist Dame Barbara Cartland's estate! From these romantic beginnings, Letitia moved to theatre school and then television stardom at the age of 11, when she was cast as Lucinda in *Grange Hill*. At 17, she lied about growing up in Hackney to land the coveted role of Sharon, Den and Angie Watts' pampered adoptive daughter. It was a part she was to play, on and off, for 20 years and which firmly fixed her in the hearts of the nation.

In between her stints on *EastEnders*, Letitia starred in *The Hello Girls* and *Lucy Sullivan Is Getting Married*, and has also appeared in *Casualty*, *The Bill*, *Doctors* and Channel 4 sitcom *Drop The Dead Donkey*. She sees *Strictly Come Dancing* as a great new challenge. 'I have always watched the show and it will be an honour to be taught by the best dancers in the world. The fact that I am involved in this series is like a surreal dream to me.'

Letitia's favourite song to dance to is 'Livin' La Vida Loca' by Ricky Martin, and she is drawn to the Rumba because it is different and quite complicated. She also fancies having a go at the Jive and the Waltz. The bubbly soap star is also a fan of the judges. 'If your bad points aren't pointed out, how do you find out where you are going wrong?' she asks. 'Sometimes you need to be criticised to learn and, from what I have seen on the programme, they are usually constructive.'

Unlike the other contestants, Letitia has not thought about winning the competition, although she thinks it would be nice to have the trophy on her mantelpiece at home. 'My goal is to achieve the ability to dance,' she comments. 'I want to make sure I walk away from the competition knowing how to dance a few routines. I would love to do well but, most importantly, I don't want to fall on my backside during the live show!'

She will be dancing with *Darren Bennett*

The Story of Series Three
A Cricketer Stumps Them All

1 Colin clears the first hurdle

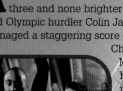

A few contestants shone from the start of series three and none brighter than presenter Zoe Ball and Olympic hurdler Colin Jackson. Zoe's debut Waltz managed a staggering score of 35 and Colin's Cha Cha Cha an amazing 32. Meanwhile Brendan found himself in the unfamiliar position of being bottom of the leader board.

2 Johnny Balls his eyes out

Presenter Johnny Ball was so proud of his lovely daughter's opening Waltz with Ian Waite, which scored an amazing 35, that he shed a tear. In the second week, the judges were getting emotional about the Brighton-based TV presenter too. 'What a glamour puss you turned out to be!' said Bruno.

3 Prince Charming fails the course

Siobhan Hayes had the briefest of visits to the *Strictly Come Dancing* team. She and partner Matthew Cutler kicked the series off with a Waltz and, for the dance, she imagined she was a lonely princess waiting by a pond, while Matthew was Prince Charming, coming to take her away. Actually, it was the audience vote that triggered her exit!

4 Dennis gets his cue

Dennis Taylor may have spent 40 years bent over a snooker table but growing up he had spent many a happy hour in the dance halls and he was confident it would all come flooding back. Partner Izabela wasn't so sure and set about improving his posture by tying his neck to a cue-like rod. His Quickstep was still compared to 'an Emperor penguin trying to hold an egg between his legs' by Bruno.

5 Brendan's bully tactics

Like a famous brand of pet food Brendan likes to win – a lot. Sadly, Fiona Phillips made every dance a dog's dinner, and that left top dog Brendan growling in frustration. Poor Fiona was on the receiving end of some very hostile behaviour after the couple's first-week Waltz. 'Brendan is being so rude,' she said as she attempted the Rumba steps. 'He looked at me as if he was going to kill me!'

6 Colin jumps for joy

Colin pulled out all the stops for his week-two Quickstep and surprised everyone when he leapt in the air and performed a high toe touch. Erin had worked him hard in training and kept telling the Olympic athlete he was too slow. But it was all worth it and the couple finished top of the board.

Colin & Erin

Zoe and Ian

Darren and Lilia

Siobhan and Matthew

Colin and Erin

Gloria and Darren

James and Camilla

Jaye and Andrew

7 'Shy' Will shows off his muscles

In week three Hanna Haarala was impressed with the army of female fans her dance partner Will Thorp attracted wherever they went. She commented that the *Casualty* star was quite shy but he didn't seem too bashful while getting a spray tan in front of the camera!

8 Gloria's star support

Gloria Hunniford went into the contest to represent the older generation. 'I'd love to be the grandmother that won it,' she said. As she practised for the Jive in week three, her best friend, Sir Cliff Richard, weighed in with a warning to the judges. 'Do not be rude to my Gloria!' he told them. Perhaps heeding Sir Cliff's message, the judges were complimentary and

Bruno gushed, 'The lady and the toy boy. Flirtatious and vivacious!' Unfortunately they only scored 19 and the public voted them out.

9 Pain and the Paso Doble

Matadors are used to injury but Colin was feeling their pain after an old knee problem flared up again. His agony wasn't going to stop Erin's training plans, though, so she issued him with a pair of knee pads! Their dance proved to be just that. 'You make a masterful matador!' said Arlene and the judges awarded a score of 31.

10 James tastes the bull-ring blood

Chef James Martin managed to put his back out when training for the Paso Doble – but his troubles didn't stop there. On the night of the dance, James faced the judges with blood pouring from his mouth and told them, 'Camilla elbowed me in the face!' But despite the injury, the dance went down well. 'I thought it had a lot of drama,' said Bruno. It certainly had that!

11 Fiona's farewell

Craig had summed up Fiona as a 'sluggish dead weight and a noose around Brendan's neck'. Then, in training for their week-four Foxtrot, Brendan thought Fiona had finally got it. But the dance, to the classic Sinatra number 'Ain't That a Kick in the Head?' turned out to be more a kick in the teeth! Craig called it 'lame!' and, after a score of 20, their best in the series, Brendan commented, 'I have never been so happy for such a lousy score.' It wasn't enough to save them this time though.

12 Colin's Casualty trip

Another week, another injury for Colin Jackson – this time a severely bruised toe. Doctors advised that he forget the training for Saturday night's Samba, but Olympians don't give up that easily. 'I'm going to have to dance through the pain' he said. Indeed, the sizzling Samba got Arlene and Bruno excited. 'The boy from Brazil let loose and bootylicious,' commented Bruno. Arlene gushed, 'You ripple and undulate with every part of your being.' Calm down, Arlene!

Dennis and Izabella

Patsy and Anton

Will and Hanna

Fiona and Brendan

Bill and Karen

13 Bill hobbles on

Colin wasn't the only one needing hospital treatment. After an ankle injury in week two, Bill Turnbull had carried on dancing but had only succeeded in making matters worse. By week five, the ankle was swollen and red causing poor Bill to come out in a horrible rash. But there's no rest for the *Strictly* contestants. His Viennese waltz was a triumph, despite the sore ankle.

14 Taylor's dummy

After insulting Dennis Taylor's Paso Doble as 'woeful', Craig was challenged to learn how to play snooker in five days and agreed to have a go. Training with Willie Thorn, Craig admitted it was 'a disaster' before facing a panel of professional snooker players. 'It was worse than woeful,' said Dennis. But the sweet taste of revenge didn't last long. After a Samba in which Len said Dennis was taken over by the 'devil of dance', he and Izabela got the cue to leave.

15 Will gets tough

Having confessed to his soldier brother that he had been taking ballet lessons, Will was in danger of being disowned, so he decided to toughen up with a spot of training. But it was too late to save the day. Will and Hanna's week-six Tango impressed Len, but Arlene didn't buy it and Bruno declared, 'It should be a torrent of passion. That was a trickle!' The public took Bruno's side and Will got his marching orders.

16 Darren's dancing dynasty

By week six, cricketer Darren Gough had picked up the dancing bug and even got his family at it. Sons Liam and Brennan were more used to sports that tripping the light fantastic, but Len gave them a lesson in Quickstep – and they loved it.

17 Temper temper!

Patsy and Anton's Cha Cha Cha to 'A Little Less Conversation' caused a heated one between Arlene and Len. 'If this had been a shimmy contest, Patsy would have won but it's not,' she sniffed. 'You're talking absolute nonsense,' replied Len and the pair traded jibes in font of a bemused Patsy. Len concluded 'The performance was much better and these three need their eyes tested.'

18 Tea but no sympathy

Having come bottom of the leader board in week six, Karen decided Bill Turnbull needed some expert help and called in dance coach Blanche, whom Bill dubbed the 'dancing mother-in-law'. 'Just when you're ready to end it all, she comes in with a lovely tray of sandwiches,' sighed Bill. The scores improved but Craig called the opening Waltz 'absolutely repulsive'. After the public vote, Bill went back to his day job.

19 A-Cha-Cha-Choo

Poor Zoe came down with flu on week eight and snuffled her way through training. 'I feel drained of all life,' complained the sickly presenter. Zoe was also upset that Erin had criticised the judges for giving her tens two weeks before, saying, 'Sorry, Zoe was great but not perfect.' But that just spurred the couple on and their second dance got a standing ovation, led by husband Norman Cook.

20 Lilia's outfit hell

Darren and Lilia suffered a setback when the strap on Lilia's dress broke in the semi-finals, but the determined dancer carried on, holding the outfit up throughout. Their combined score of 64 for the Waltz and Samba left them trailing second to last. Colin's Waltz was praised by Craig but it was Zoe and Ian who impressed the judges the most. They went through to the final at the top of the leader board.

21 James's romantic Rumba

Despite rumours of a budding relationship between James and Camilla, the shy chef was struggling with the romantic nature of the Rumba. The Foxtrot won the couple praise all round, and a score of 33, but the Rumba fell flat. 'You went from Fred Astaire to Freddy Krueger,' said Bruno. After the public had their say, James and Camilla waltzed off into the sunset.

22 Perfect partners

For the final, Zoe and Ian repeated the success of their unforgettable Tango with another two tens and considerable praise. 'Emotional, dramatic,' said Arlene. 'What they were doing on the floor was floor play!' 'What a blockbuster. Love, sex, drama!' raved Bruno, and Craig called it 'absolutely savage'. But Zoe and Ian were the first to be voted out by the public.

23 Colin's dummy dance

Athlete Colin Jackson appeared to be racing for the finish line as his first dance of the final, the Quickstep, scored a massive 39 points, and Colin was reduced to tears by the three tens he was awarded. His Rumba wasn't bad either and Arlene praised his work with Erin Boag as 'a perfect partnership'. But Colin fell at the final hurdle when the show dance, involving two full-sized puppets, appalled the judges. 'This belonged to an end of pier entertainment not an *SCD* final,' sniffed Bruno.

24 Darren's a winner

Darren's last three dances showed just how far he'd come from the clumsy cricketer of week one. The Foxtrot earned him a ten from Len, who said it was 'wonderful' and the Paso Doble had Arlene calling him 'one proud, hunky matador'. With a score of 72, Darren and Lilia finished bottom of the leader board but the *pièce de résistance* was yet to come. A triumphant show dance had Craig declaring, 'Like Bisto you saved the best 'til last.' After bowling the public over, Darren and Lilia lifted the series-three trophy.

Some might choose to do *Strictly Come Dancing* to learn a new skill or to raise their profile. Darren Gough did it to please his mum! The Yorkshire and England cricketer initially had no intention of swapping his whites for a sequinned shirt. 'When they first asked me, I thought, "You must be joking! Not a chance!" Then I told my mum about it and she was so excited. She really wanted me to do it so I said I would, just to please my mum!'

And Mum wasn't the only member of the family cheering the Barnsley lad on. Plain-speaking Yorkshire lass Granny Gough became a regular fixture on the show, dishing out advice and encouragement to her grandson, and Darren even took partner Lilia Kopylova home to meet her. 'Don't take any notice of the judges,' said Connie Gough. 'You keep it up. Do your best, darling, for Nana.' Having been a cricketer for 18 years, Darren was also in for some serious ribbing from his team-mates when they discovered he was taking part in *Strictly Come Dancing*. But he decided to face the music – and dance. And he invited them along to watch.

In week one, Darren danced the Cha Cha Cha to the Donna Summer hit 'Hot Stuff'. Sadly, the judges didn't think the song was referring to his dance style and Craig called him 'chunky and lumpy'. 'The frightening thing,' says Darren, 'was that I was doing something I had never done before, and doing something that I didn't think was very macho. But when I turned up to practise the Quickstep in week two, I had Robbie Williams' music and a quick, lively dance which was more me. I really loved it. Then we had the Tango, followed by the Paso Doble, which I also liked, so those three weeks got me really involved and I got the bug for dance.' It seems the bug was infectious and Darren soon had his two sons practising ballroom with Len Goodman. 'Len gave the two boys a lesson and they loved it,' he says. 'I was so proud watching them dance.'

By week three, Darren had the judges eating out of his much criticised 'bowling hands', with Bruno dubbing him 'the Yorkshire Valentino'. And he soon became living proof that you can be as macho as you like and still trip the light fantastic. Having declared he felt 'a right Charlie' while practising for the week-eight Rumba, he impressed Len with his masculine take on the dance. 'You are a proper geezer,' enthused the jubilant judge. 'You dance like a bloke.' The semi-final brought mixed emotions for Darren and Lilia with a triumphant Waltz and a Samba which was nearly ruined when the strap on Lilia's dress broke and she had to finish the dance with one arm across her chest to stop the top slipping down.

By this time, the public were well and truly on Darren's side and were determined to see what he could do in the final. They weren't disappointed. His slow Foxtrot earned him his first perfect ten, and his Paso Doble had Arlene gasping, 'You were great. One proud, hunky matador!' Then came

'You were great. One proud, hunky matador!'

the *pièce de résistance* – the show dance. 'You could tell I was nervous when I started and there were some really complex moves in there,' recalls Darren. In the end, Colin and Erin beat them with the judges' scores but

Darren and Lilia left with the trophy after the public voted on the back of his incredible journey from stumbling sportsman to whirling dervish. 'Colin was a great dancer but I think the public liked that I had never danced before and that I enjoyed it,' says Darren.

'The show hasn't changed my life and I still do pretty well at cricket. But more people recognise me, especially women, and people want to talk about dancing instead of cricket. But that's fine by me – I've been talking about cricket for the last 18 years!'

Darren on …

Mark Ramprakash
Ramps was probably one of the best dancers from week one and he likes dancing – I've seen him do it in nightclubs. With me it was different. I really enjoyed ballroom dancing but disco dancing? Nah

The High Point
The high point was getting through the Jive. It was a fast routine and the backing group played it a bit too quickly. But I pulled it off and it was amazing in the end.

The Low Point
Week one, when I got that cut-off shirt! I thought I'd be out week one or two, so at the costume fitting I said, 'Just get me whatever,' so I ended up with that shirt!

Facing the Judges
It's not very nice but they're there to entertain the public so you know that, unless you are the best one or two of the night, you are going to get a hard time from them. I have respect for them because they are professionals in what they do. But if they tried to play cricket, I'd absolutely slaughter them, because they'd be rubbish!

The Fearsome, Foursome

Arlene Phillips' style of judging is a bit like a faulty air-conditioning unit – it blows hot and cold at a moment's notice. One of the country's leading choreographers, she rarely minces her words when it comes to the poorer dancers on the show, but she has been known to get hot under the collar for some of the sexier males, notably series four winner Mark Ramprakash.

'I lose all perspective when I watch you dance,' she commented, after Mark's week-three Tango. And after Matt Dawson disappointed her with his Tango in the semi-final, she declared, 'I just want raw sex!' In return, Matt quipped, 'I think it's obvious what Arlene wants – and she's just said it on national television!'

But while she is appreciative of the great dancers, she is equally harsh to those who fall below par. Poor Fiona Phillips (no relation!) got the sharp end of her tongue on day one of series three, when she said her Waltz with Brendan was 'so awful I don't know what to say', and Quentin Willson's Cha Cha Cha 'makes Chris Parker look like a ten.' But Arlene, who proudly states she 'makes no allowances for anyone', doesn't regret a single word. 'I think I'm firm rather than harsh,' she says. 'Firm, honest and direct. I've always been that way. It's just my style.'

The Manchester-born choreographer, and creative force behind the risqué dance group Hot Gossip, started dancing at

lene

'Firm, honest and direct. I've always been that way. It's just my style.'

Arlene on …

Meeting Bruno
I was teaching Jazz at a dance centre in London and he was here doing a show. He came into my class and talked from the first day, so I had to notice him, and he never stopped. We've worked together a lot since and the relationship is great – until he does my head in by talking too much!

The Other Judges
I love them, even when I'm on the show with them. Craig is as mean as he looks. He's not got a good word to say!

Favourite Dancer of All Time
It has to be Fred Astaire. He was so fleet of foot that it looked like his feet never touched the ground. Beautiful.

the age of three before attending the austere-sounding Muriel Tweedy School of Dancing. 'I did as many classes as my parents could afford,' she reveals. 'That's what I wanted to do and I didn't want anything else in my life.' And her own dance training may go some way to explain her direct manner of criticism, as harsh words were the order of the day. 'When I was dancing, that's the way everyone was taught,' recalls Arlene. 'Nobody had a nice word to say about anyone. My life was one of constant criticism and that's the way dancers were taught. Nobody was politically correct – you told people exactly what you thought of them and that's the way it was.' As well as the verbal threats there was also the stick, which would appear when anyone displayed 'naughty feet'. 'We would get a tap if we weren't doing something right – not relentlessly, but you knew it was there.'

Arlene started her career as a dancer but quickly became respected in the world of choreography, working on pop videos for artists such as George Michael, Queen and Aretha Franklin. As well as masterminding Hot Gossip, she choreographed hit West End musicals, including *Grease*, *Saturday Night Fever* and *We Will Rock You*. Her films include *Annie* and Monty Python's *The Meaning of Life*. Throughout

her illustrious career, however, she has been more impressed by dedication than star quality. 'Elton John and Freddie Mercury are the two most inspiring people I've worked with,' she says. 'You can recognise their talents without question and both were committed. I respect people that work hard.'

Nonetheless, she realises that, while everybody on *Strictly Come Dancing* works hard to learn their dances, some may be a lost cause! 'Some people cannot send the message from the brain to the rest of the body and that has nothing whatsoever to do with intellect,' she explains. 'It's just that the body doesn't recognise the message. You can see it in children from an early age; those kids who never learn to skip, they never have that natural rhythm which comes so easily to some. If you have that natural ability to skip and keep in time with the music and identify with the music, then you've got a head start.' And there are no surprises when Arlene names the two celebrities whom she thinks probably couldn't skip when they were kids! 'Fiona Phillips was probably the worst,' she says. 'It's either Fiona or Quentin Willson. They just couldn't hack it at all!'

Strictly's Biggest Surprise
I think probably Mark Ramprakash made the biggest leap because he'd had no formal dance experience whatsoever. He turned out to be such a wonderful dancer, so I think he was the biggest surprise.

Kenny Logan is more at home on a rugby pitch than a dance floor and admits he's no Fred Astaire. In fact, when he was younger, he was so worried he would embarrass himself at discos, he used to fake rugby injuries to get out of dancing with the girls!

Kenny Logan

Strictly Come Dancing, however, is a chance to put his shyness behind him, for the sake of his wife and fellow contestant, Gabby Logan. 'She really wanted me to do it and I thought it would be great to learn a new skill,' he says. 'I might not be the best dancer ever but I'm not afraid to embarrass myself in front of millions of people!'

The last time Kenny danced was at the couple's 2001 wedding, in the Scottish town of Blairlogie, where he told Gabby he would 'only do it the once'. Even so, being a naturally competitive sportsman, Kenny is determined to go home with the famous mirror ball trophy. 'You shouldn't be in it if you don't want to win it,' he comments. 'I'd definitely love to win.'

The Scottish player began his career at Stirling County Rugby Club, helping them to win the Scottish League Championship in 1995/1996. The following season, he joined the London Wasps, where he stayed for seven years. In the summer of 2004 he signed for Glasgow and in September 2005 made his debut for London Scottish.

He will be dancing with Ola Jordan

At an international level, Kenny gained his first cap for Scotland against Australia in 1992, at the age of 20. He went on to play for Scotland in the 1999 Five Nations Championship and the IRB Rugby World Cups of 1995, 1999 and 2003 (making the quarter-finals on each occasion). Having won 70 caps over 13 years, he retired from international rugby union after the 2003 World Cup. He now runs his own hospitality company and provides rugby commentary on ITV.

Although his dance experience is limited, Kenny never shies away from a challenge and has overcome huge difficulties in the past. Diagnosed with a severe form of dyslexia, he received successful treatment from the Dore Programme and now attends conferences and writes articles to help parents and teachers tackle the condition. But he describes himself as a lover, not a dancer, and admits that when he dances, onlookers often laugh so much he has to stop!

However, the six-foot-one player, who has two-year-old twins with Gabby, is taking his inspiration from friend and fellow rugby player Matt Dawson. 'I watched the last series and I thought it was brilliant,' he says. 'I wanted Matt to win but I also supported Mark, because I thought he was great from the beginning and deserved to go all the way.'

And, if his Samba looks like a scrum, the burly Scot won't mind the scathing comments from the judges. 'I'm used to criticism from rugby coaches,' he says. 'I think it spurs me on and makes me better.'

'I might not be the best dancer ever but I'm not afraid to embarrass myself in front of millions of people!'

Smillie, Spice and the Schmeichel shake

1 Putting on the Ritz

For series four, things changed again, with 14 celebrities competing over 12 weeks. Cutting a dash in top hat and tails, newsreader Nicholas Owen certainly looked the part for his week-one Waltz with Nicole Cutler. Sadly, it didn't cut the mustard with the judges. 'Hat, why bother?' Craig said. 'Waltz, why bother?' Ouch! Nick and Nic were out.

2 Jimmy bows out

Comedian Jimmy Tarbuck claimed he was 'clumsier than a warthog' when he signed up for the show. His Waltz was dismissed as 'absolutely average' by Craig, and Jimmy never got another chance to prove himself as he was forced to withdraw for health reasons.

3 A partnership made in hell

For their debut Rumba, Georgina Bouzova and James Jordan chose the Marvin Gaye track 'Let's Get It On', but they certainly weren't getting on in training. The slim *Casualty* actress was upset when James told her she could do with losing a few pounds and his bullying tactics soon had her in tears.

4 Bad boy meets bad girl!

Masterful Brendan Cole was in for a shock when he met his new dance partner, former *Bad Girls* star Clare King. 'It's not often I come across women who can overpower me,' he laughed. But the pair's raunchy Rumba was marked down by the judges after Brendan included an illegal lift which left Arlene and Len fuming.

5 Ray of sunshine

Ray Fearon's week-one Cha Cha Cha had been a hit with the judges, but daughter Rosa had a problem with her dad's 'frog hands'. Rosa popped along to the Tango training to show the *Coronation Street* actor what she meant.

6 Oh no you don't!

After last week's poor score, Clare King was concerned she was losing her power over Brendan, who refused to listen to her pleas to drop the lifts from the Jive routine. But on the night the lady got her way – as Brendan went to lift her up, Clare shook her head and wagged her finger. The judges loved the cheeky move.

 Georgina and James

 Matt and Lilia

 Emma and Darren

 Ray and Camila

 Clare and Brendan

 Nicholas and Nicole

 Louisa and Vincent

7 Louisa's tears of joy

Youngest ever contestant Louisa Lytton was in for a treat with her Italian dance partner Vincent Simone. 'I am a passionate person and with Louisa I am going to be quite flirty,' he confessed. Their Jive was a triumph and Louisa's number one fan, Bruno, awarded them a ten, reducing the emotional girl to tears. With a great score of 36, they finished on top.

8 Spoony knifed

After seeing his straight-faced Tango with Ola Jordan, Len predicted great things for cheeky DJ Spoony in the Latin dances and they gained a respectable score of 27. Even so, viewers didn't get the chance to see the smile return to his face because of his shock elimination in the public vote.

9 Jan's not laughing now

At the start of the series, comedienne Jan Raven was worried that she and partner Anton du Beke were having too much fun. By week four, the laughter had turned to tears, as the pressure got too much for Jan and she stormed out.

10 Hello down there

Not the most elegant of sportsmen at the start, Peter Schmeichel really struggled with the Paso Doble in week four. Partner Erin Boag called in old friend Ian Waite, who had been knocked out in week one, to demonstrate how height could be turned into dynamism. Unfortunately the coaching had little effect and they ended bottom of the board.

11 No gentleman Jim

Tempers flared in Georgina's training, too, as James continued with his cruel-to-be-kind approach. Georgina complained that they were wasting too much time arguing, James replied. 'So shut your mouth and listen!' Charming. The couple scored 26 for their dance but the public saved Georgina from more torment by voting them out.

12 Disaster for Mark and Karen

Mark Ramprakash and Karen Hardy were riding high in week four and their Salsa promised to be hot, hot hot! On the night, disaster struck! Karen was devastated when she had to stop because the couple had got tangled together with a microphone wire. But Mark appealed for another go and got one. The Salsa sizzled and the couple led the board again.

Peter and Erin

Mica and Ian

Spoony and Ola

Mark and Karen

Jan and Anton

Carol and Matthew

Jimmy and Flavia

13 Lilia drafts in some support

Rugby player Matt Dawson went all shy when it came to the Salsa. He refused to touch Lilia's bottom because she wasn't his girlfriend – so Lilia brought the real one in. Former Miss Northern Ireland, Joanne Salley, tried to show Matt how to get saucy. Arlene sensed his reticence in the dance, saying, 'You have sensuality, but you don't explode. Something is holding you back.'

14 Louisa gets tough

'No guts, no glory' was Louisa's motto of the week after she spent some time in a boxing gym bearing the legend. 'Craig, if you want attack, I'll give you attack,' promised the tiny firecracker.

15 Camilla's carnival surprise

Ray Fearon struggled to find his fiesta spirit in training for the Samba, so Camilla laid on a surprise carnival show. The actor soon got into the swing of things, but the result was disappointing. 'Camilla, you were hot,' said Arlene. 'Ray, you were not.' A score of 26 saw them second to bottom, above Peter Schmeichel, but the goalie saved himself and Ray said goodbye.

16 Don't cry for me …

Louisa may be an actress but she found it difficult to get into character for the intense Tango, because she kept laughing, so Vincent took her for a night at the theatre. After watching the hot-blooded drama of *Evita*, Louisa got a bit hot and heavy with the production's John Clarke, who showed her his fancy footwork. It did the trick. She stopped giggling and delivered a terrific Tango and landed a score of 35.

17 The Schmeichel shake

In week six, Peter and Erin had chosen Odyssey's 'Shake Your Body Down' as their Samba song and the Schmeichel shake was born. Having caught on all over the country, Peter even managed to get a smile out of Anne Robinson when he got her shaking her body down on *The Weakest Link*. Week seven's show coincided with his birthday, but there were no happy returns for Peter as the public voted him off.

18 Matt's jumping Jive

Matt may have started the series with a measly 19 for his Cha Cha Cha but by week seven he had made it to the top of the leader board. The improvement was amazing so it's no wonder that Lilia encouraged Matt to kick over her head during the Jive. The judges loved it, but with 28 points, they lost poll position to Mark and Karen.

19 · Training with attitude

Clare was clearly a bad influence on Brendan as her idea of Samba training was to drag him to the stables and then to the pub! They may have regretted the time out when Bruno told them, 'It was like a drunk Samba the morning after at an 18-30 club!.' Clare's likeable nature wasn't enough to save them from the public vote, so they rode into the sunset.

20 · Emma adds some spice

Baby Spice rocked on the night. Her Waltz had Craig 'absolutely mesmerised' and Emma jumped for joy as she received two tens and a score of 37. The Paso Doble achieved the same score with one ten from Bruno and gave Craig goosebumps. With a top score of 74, no one was more surprised than Emma to find herself in the bottom two after the public vote.

21 · Carol's swan song

As show nine approached, *Changing Rooms* star and mother-of-three Carol Smillie started to feel her age. 'I've got twenty years on both the other girls and I'm feeling it,' she said. Score-wise, this was to be her most triumphant night. After Arlene commented on the second dance with 'what a sexy Samba sizzler!', a delighted Carol rushed over to hug her. But another score of 34 couldn't save her.

22 · Christmas cheer

Christmas was in the air and Emma's tough training was brightened up by a very welcome visit from her niece and nephew, bearing seasonal gifts, and the magic rubbed off. Their Tango won them a score of 36 and their Salsa 33, and Craig called them 'absolutely phenomenal'. Even so, Baby Spice was back in the rack after the public vote.

23 · Laurels and Hardy

Mark's competitive nature had him turning the tables on Karen Hardy and making her train nine hours a day. 'He's killing me,' said the super-fit dancer. After a fantastic Quickstep, the couple moved on to a triumphant Tango which knocked them dead. Arlene called them 'magnetic'. When three perfect scores came up, Karen was in floods of tears and the couple went into the final in the top position.

24 · Batsman at his best

The blood, sweat and copious tears were all worth it when Karen and Mark got to the final. The Salsa was sensational, earning them a perfect score of 40, and their Show Dance made Len 'want to shout'. They even got a standing ovation from the judges! The tears were flowing again as the deserving couple lifted the trophy, and ladies all over the country sighed at the thought of Saturday nights without their fix of hot hips Ramprakash.

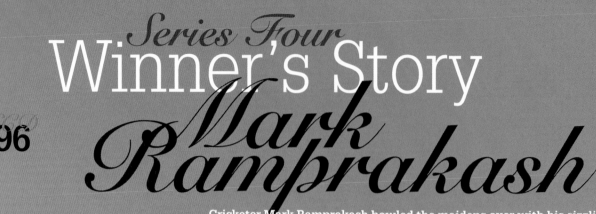

Series Four
Winner's Story
Mark Ramprakash

Cricketer Mark Ramprakash bowled the maidens over with his sizzling Salsa and his sexy Samba, and even brought a flush to tough cookie Arlene's cheeks. But, after 20 years as a professional cricketer and top batsman for England, Middlesex and Surrey, Mark was initially reluctant to swap the wicket for the Waltz. 'It took me a while to think about it,' he says. 'Darren Gough had done so well by winning the series before, but he is a very different personality. He's very out there and confident. We had a chat and he told me how much he had enjoyed it and he said, "Go for it!"'

Mark, who was 37 when he was asked to take part in the show, decided the time had come to explore new avenues. 'I was coming to the twilight of my career,' he recalls. 'I thought I should start being a bit more open to doing other things, so I went home and told my family I was going to do it. My wife, Van, and daughter, Cara, had watched Darren in series three and had loved it, so Van was very excited. Cara burst out laughing!'

The Mark that wowed his way to the trophy in the final was a far cry from the shy, nervous cricketer that we saw in week one. Dance partner Karen Hardy certainly thought she had a challenge ahead. 'I opened the door to this shy, reserved gentleman and thought, "What am I going to do? There's no way he will perform those dances and wear all those sequinned outfits." But when I saw him move, I knew I had to keep pushing him.'

During the tough weeks of training, leading up to the first dance, Karen struggled to teach him the Cha Cha Cha, complaining, 'He's just so nice. I can't get any fire out of him!' As the first live show approached, Mark really found his feet but he admits his nerves were harder to conquer than the fancy footwork. 'I was much more nervous than I have ever been at cricket,' shudders Mark. 'It was the hardest thing I've ever done. The build-up doesn't help. You get to the studio in the morning and you don't go on until six in the evening – and knowing it's live

'Once again you
ignited my fire.
That was fantastic!'

makes it so much worse. I was really worried I was going to make a mistake. But no one wants to go out in the first round, so I managed to get out there and do it and give it my best.' The performance obviously belied the butterflies in his tummy, as Bruno declared, 'You are Mr Confidence!' Even craggy Craig enthused about his cheeky Cha Cha Cha. 'At last we have someone who can actually move and use the floor,' he said. 'Thank God!'

After finishing top of the leader board, along with Ray Fearon and DJ Spoony, the next few weeks saw a steady improvement in Mark's confidence, with some thrilling dance displays and one of our esteemed judges getting very hot under the collar! 'I lose all perspective when you dance,' declared Arlene after the week-three Tango. And the following week's Paso Doble had her smouldering. 'Once again you ignited my fire,' she sizzled. 'That was fantastic! Taut buttocks! You have it all!'

Disaster struck in week five when the couple's Salsa became the first dance in *Strictly Come Dancing*'s history to be stopped. Mark's microphone got tangled in Karen's dress and the couple were unable to carry on. 'That was horrendous,' Mark recalls. 'It was like it took place in slow motion. It seemed like the band played on

for ages before someone told them to stop. Karen was desperately upset but I didn't know that in a professional competition no one gets a second chance, so I just spontaneously said, "Can we have another go please?" and they let us.' Despite the knock-back the Salsa was a sensation. 'You turned a meltdown into a triumph,' gushed Bruno, as Len declared it 'the best Salsa of the night'. But even the score of 36 didn't entirely repair the damage. 'It affected both of us much more than we realised at the time,' reveals Mark. 'It really knocked our confidence for the next couple of weeks.'

Determination, as ever, won through and the semi-final saw the couple's Argentine Tango win the votes of judges and viewers alike. Arlene called the dance 'magnetic, electric', and Craig said, 'One word: a-ma-zing!' As Tess commented that they were the only couple to have got through to the semi-finals without a perfect ten, the judges responded by giving them three tens and a score of 39. The final saw the hardworking couple perform five sensational dances, including the Salsa, which gained them a perfect score of 40 from the judges. Their show dance had the audience and the judges on their feet in a standing ovation. 'Like the song says, you make me want to shout!' said Len. 'That was fantastic.' Even runner-up Matt Dawson was full of praise. 'There's no question there was one winner here,' he said. 'That was FINAL!'

Sadly, the dashing sportsman, who danced his way into a nation's heart, has hardly danced since that heart-stopping final, as he's been more intent on scoring

> ## Their show dance had the audience and the judges on their feet in a standing ovation

runs than judges' points. 'It was the experience of a lifetime and I really enjoyed it,' Mark says. 'It's great to have an opportunity to learn new dances but I haven't danced since the show. Perhaps once the cricket season is over!' Nonetheless, the show has brought him a whole new fan base – most of whom are probably female! 'So people say!' says the bashful batsman. 'It has put me in the limelight, so, when I travel on the train to cricket matches, I am recognised by all sorts of people now.' He adds, 'Essentially, I'm back in my day job, but dancing comes up every day and I do get the odd "twinkle toes" comment from the crowd! We've had lots of fan mail from different people too – a lot of them children, who draw pictures of Karen in her pink dress dancing with me. It's really sweet.'

But one young fan has a special reason to remember the show with pride – Mark's nine-year-old daughter Cara. 'She does dance classes and I visited her school on the show, so that was nice for her,' Mark says. 'She was definitely more into *Strictly Come Dancing* than cricket. She's only interested in cricket if there's an ice-cream machine at the ground!'

Mark on …

Favourite Dance
I loved the Salsa because it's less formal than the ballroom dances. It's very free and loose and there are not many rules.

Worst Dance
Any ballroom dance! You have to remember your footwork and your arms, keeping your back straight and your head back – and smile at the same time!

Worst Training Week
The Rumba because it's so slow. Some of the other dances, like the Quickstep or Paso Doble, are very fast so you just throw yourself into it but I was really nervous about performing the Rumba.

Karen
I am so lucky to have had Karen as a teacher. She has a fabulous personality and it brought out the best in me. She started off a bit tough, like a Sergeant Major, but as I progressed she got more flexible. She is a brilliant teacher and we've become good friends, and she even comes along to the odd cricket match with her husband and little boy.

'I'm looking forward to the Salsa as I love to wiggle. I love to let my hair down and really let go '

Penny Lancaster-Stewart can't wait to show off her 'Hot Legs' on the SCD set. After watching the last series, the freelance photographer, and wife of rock legend Rod Stewart, wanted to take up dance lessons again. 'When I was younger, I did tap, ballet and modern,' she says. 'But I gave it up when I was 12 and haven't had a lesson since. I love the way that *Strictly Come Dancing* has taken something that was seen as old-fashioned and made it fun and exciting again.'

Penny Lancaster Stewart

Penny started her career as a model, starring in TV commercials for After Eights and Ferrero Rocher, among others. At the height of her career, she decided to take a two-year course in photography and, during her first year, she was invited to photograph Rod, after asking him for an autograph. Rod then followed this up with a request for a date - some eight months later!

In November 2005, the couple had a son, Alastair, and in June 2007, after seven years together, they shared a romantic wedding in the Italian Riviera. For their first dance as a married couple, Penny hired a choreographer to help with their dance to the appropriately named 'At Last' by Eta James. 'I wasn't sure that Rod would go for it but he really enjoyed it, even though on the day he almost let me go during one of the back holds. The whole thing was very surreal.'

Although she is a young mum, fitness won't be an issue for Penny, who is a qualified instructor and recently produced her own exercise video. She has always loved dancing but admits she was terrified of performing as a youngster. 'When I was at school we had to go to auditions at the local theatre,' she says. 'I hated being in the spotlight and would refuse to go.'

Since signing up to the show, she has worried that the familiar stage fright might return. 'I'm worried that I'll freeze and go blank during the live shows and forget the steps,' she says. 'And I'm scared that I'll fall over and drag my dance partner down with me!'

When it comes to the judges, Penny feels her former career as a model will stand her in good stead. 'I think positive criticism is really healthy and helps you to improve,' she says. 'I got used to negative criticism when I was working in the modelling world.'

A hopeless romantic, Penny loves the Fred and Ginger films and thinks she will enjoy the elegant ballroom dances. But it seems there's a wild side too. 'I'm looking forward to the Salsa as I love to wiggle,' she laughs. 'I love to let my hair down and really let go. The faster dances may be less nerve-racking because the adrenaline rush will mean I won't have to concentrate as much.'

As for the dresses, at six-feet-one, with legs to die for, she's bound to wear them well!

She will be dancing with Ian Waite

102

THE JIVE

The Jive became a huge craze in America in the 1920s and was frowned upon by older traditionalists, which made it even more popular with the young. The GIs brought it to the UK during the war and in the 1950s it was danced to rock and roll tracks in dance halls everywhere.

The Jive is all about kicks and flicks, so it's perfect for a high-energy workout. Keep it fast and furious and enjoy it!

Move 1
Front Kicks

1

2

- Stretch your arms above your head and go up on to your toes
  With a little jump, kick your right leg straight out in front (1)
- Bring the leg back, jump and kick with the left leg (2)

Move 2
Back Kicks

- Stand with feet together and bend the knees (1)
- Kick the left leg backwards, pointing your toes (2)
- Bring your feet together and kick the right foot back (3)
- Try single then double kicks on each side

Move 3
Low Side Kick

1

2

- Bend your right leg at the knee **(1)**
- Kick out to the side, at a 45 degree angle from your standing leg **(2)**

From there go into:

Move 4
The Grapevine

1

2

3

4

- Cross your right leg behind your left **(1)**
- Step left **(2)**
- Put right foot in front of left **(3)**
- Bring left leg into a low kick **(4)**
- Repeat in the opposite direction

Move 5
Two Stage Kick

1   2

- Do two low kicks to the right
- Raise the same leg as high as is comfortable, with a bent knee **(1)**
- Kick twice from the knee **(2)**
- Repeat on the other side and put a grapevine in between when you are ready

Move 6
Chicken Walks

1   2

- Lean your upper body back and place your hands on your hips, with arms slightly back so that they resemble chicken wings. Stretch your right foot in front of you with toes pointed **(1)**
- Walk forward, pointing alternate feet in front and leading with the opposite arm **(2)**

Step Tap

1

2

3

- Tap your left foot behind your right **(1)**
- Kick low to the right
- Tap behind again and kick higher **(2)**
- Repeat twice more, raising your leg each time **(3)**
- Repeat on the other side

THE JIVE

Toe Heel Cross

- Tap your right toes next to your left foot **(1)**
- Straighten your leg and tap your heel **(2)**
- Cross the right foot over the left leg **(3)**
- Tap with left toes close to right leg **(4)**
- Tap with left heel **(5)**
- Cross left foot over right **(6)**
- When you have mastered that, add a kick on each side

Cooling down and stretching after a workout is every bit as important as the warm up. These exercises will bring your heart rate down and will help to prevent muscle injury, so don't be tempted to skip them.

The Cucaracha

- Stand with your weight on your left leg, ready to move to your right

- With right arm outstretched, take a step to the side with your right leg and transfer your weight, while your left foot stays in the same place

- Bring your right foot in and place it close to your left, bringing your arm in again and transferring your weight back to the left leg. Repeat the process, moving to the left

Botafogos with Hip Rolls

- Start facing diagonally and step forward onto a bent right leg.

- Bring left foot forward with partial weight transfer, making a quarter turn to the right

- Straighten the right leg and roll the hips

- Repeat in the opposite direction

DOWN

COOL DOWN

Botafogos with Body Ripples

- Perform the Botafogo as above

- Now, with arms outstretched, push chest out

- Lean back and push your stomach out

- Now move upper body forward, while pushing your bottom backwards and sinking into your legs

Check Step

- Cross your right foot over your left

- Tap to the side and cross left foot over right. Repeat in sets of eight

Squat Stretch

- Bend upper body and squat down with arms loose

- Straighten your whole body up and stretch out to the sides

Side Stretch

- With your feet apart, stretch your right leg out to the side, keeping the left leg bent

- Stretch your right arm above your head and lean to the left

- Now lunge to the right, bending your right leg and stretching your left

- As you progress, take it a little further down

- Repeat on the other side

Stationary Samba with Stretch

- Walk diagonally forward for four steps, starting with your right leg. Make sure you use those hips!

- Bring your right foot forward, bend the knee and stretch the left leg to the side

- Samba backwards for four steps and stretch the right leg to the side

Leg Stretch

- Bend your right knee and straighten your left leg behind you, in a lunge. Stretch your arms above your head and lean forward

- Repeat on the other side

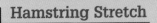

Hamstring Stretch

- Kneel down with your body upright and your knees at a 90° angle

- Stretch your right leg out to the side

- No turn your body towards your outstretched leg and point toes upwards

- Bend your upper body over your leg until you feel the stretch up your hamstring

- Repeat on the other side

Side Stretch

- Still kneeling, stretch your right leg out to the side, raise your right hand towards the ceiling and lean to the left

- Repeat on the other side

Yoga Stretch

- Get down on all fours then sit on your heels, stretching your arms out in front of you

RELAX!

Following in the dainty footsteps of pal Louisa Lytton, Matt Di Angelo is the latest actor to make the journey from Albert Square to *Strictly Come Dancing*. 'I came to watch Louisa a couple of times in the last series,' says the *EastEnders* star. 'I was impressed with the amount of effort everyone had put in, and I enjoyed watching them because they all looked as if they were having a laugh.'

Matt Di Angelo

Matt, who is best known as Deano in the BBC soap, trained at the Sylvia Young Theatre School before embarking on a career in acting and modelling. He was working in a shoe shop when he discovered he had landed the role of wide-boy Deano Wicks and, within weeks, he was a household name. Female fans of *Strictly Come Dancing* are also in for a treat, as Matt was nominated Sexiest Male in the 2006 British Soap Awards.

But good looks and theatre training doesn't necessarily mean he'll cut it on the dance floor. He admits to shying away from dance classes at school and, at aged 20, his experience of ballroom is limited. 'To be honest, I don't know the difference between ballroom and Latin,' he confesses. 'But I think it will be fun finding out.' A big fan of Justin Timberlake, hip hop and R&B, Matt does occasionally enjoy a boogie at a party – most recently on a beach – and has even put on an impromptu busking session. 'I was out with

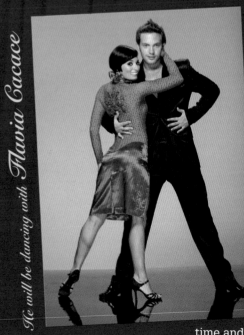

He will be dancing with Flavia Cacace

a friend, who is a dancer, and we were in the mood for a laugh,' he remembers. 'We started dancing, doing street dance moves. All of a sudden there was a circle of people watching us. It was like something out of *Saturday Night Fever*.'

Things didn't go quite as well when he was at school, however, especially when he attended a ballet class. He was told to wear a dance support, which he duly donned, only to be met with howls of laughter when he walked into class. No one told him he had to wear his support *underneath* his trousers!

Unlike his screen character, whose backchat frequently lands him in hot water, Matt vows to take the judges' comments on the chin. 'It's ignorant not to listen to someone who knows more about something than you do,' he says.

A devoted Arsenal fan, he also plays football himself, so he has the advantage of being young and fit, which will help him through the tough training, and he is determined to put 100 per cent into the show. 'I'm here to have a good time, and try something new,' he says. 'And I believe that if you put in enough time and effort, then you shouldn't be scared to fail.'

It remains to be seen whether the soap star, who follows four former *EastEnders* stars on the show, is more Jill Halfpenny than Chris Parker. And he doesn't seem overly optimistic: 'I think it would be nice to win,' he smiles, 'but I doubt I will.'

'We started dancing, doing street dance moves. All of a sudden there was a circle of people watching us. It was like something out of *Saturday Night Fever* '

The Strictly Unofficial Awards

Most Astonishing Transformation

Matt Dawson, who went from klutz to Gene Kelly in the shortest space of time. His Cha Cha Cha in the first week of series four was met with a grim response from the judges. Craig called it 'dull, dull, dull' and added, 'I was bored to tears.' But by week six, he had Arlene gasping, 'What a revelation! From boring to brilliant in six weeks!' After his Quickstep in week ten, Craig said, 'Matt, in this competition you are the one who has grown the most from then to now. Fantastic.'

Least Flattering Outfit

Lesley Garrett's 'Tequila Sunrise' dress.
The accomplished opera singer could have been renamed Lesley Garish for donning this yellow, orange and pink creation. The fringe splayed out so much during spins that Bruce commented, 'You look like a carwash!' and Craig said, 'I think the dress did all the work.'

Best Lift

Mark and Karen's final show dance.
Mark showed his muscle and proved he was king of the dance floor when he span Karen round and hoisted her up above his head in the couple's series four final show dance. Bruno called the routine, 'The crowning glory on a spectacular night' and Arlene said, 'Most dancers couldn't do those lifts in 16 years, let alone 16 weeks. Amazing.'

Most Incredible Hairstyle

Lesley Garrett's hairstyle with a
huge butterfly clip in series one.
Diva Lesley Garrett seemed to be
wearing someone else's hair for the Cha
Cha Cha in series one. Some clever work
with hair extensions left her with
this flattering look – although
they didn't quite match her own hair colour.

Steamiest Clinch

The end of **Claire Sweeney** and John
Byrnes's Rumba, which they finished too close
for comfort, leading Bruce to tell them, 'Break
it up, break it up!'

Understatement of the Show

Brendan: 'I'm very competitive.'

Dances Most Like a Dad at a Wedding

David Dickinson

David's fumbling footwork and the addition of his famous 'jazz hands'
invoked that cringe-making moment when the rhythmically challenged
relative asks you to dance at a family do. Time to head to the bar!

Most Steps Wrong in A Dance

Diarmuid Gavin's Cha Cha Cha in series two. He may know when to plant his bulbs and prune his roses, but remembering dance moves clearly wasn't Diarmuid's forte. His series two Cha Cha Cha was a series of stumbles rather than steps.

Most Argumentative Competitor

David Dickinson, who constantly argued with poor Camilla in series one. At one point he told her, 'What you have to do is be a little more tolerant,' before complaining, 'You're not explaining it to me simply!' 'I'm trying, David,' said an exasperated Camilla. And so was he – *very* trying!

Pushiest Professional

James Jordan, when training with Georgina Bouzova in series four. After telling Georgina she could do with losing a pound or two, James reduced her to tears with his constant criticism. When she lost it, he exclaimed, 'Weak, weak, weak. I have no time for crying.' Poor Georgina!

Best Brucie Insult

'Diarmuid knows he has to lead with his left foot – he just doesn't know which one!'

Weirdest Analogy From a Judge

Bruno describing Peter Schmeichel's Samba in series four:
'It was like a brazil nut at a stag party; only the shell was left on the floor.'

Best at Dancing Through the Pain

Bill Turnbull who had a sprained, then infected ankle, then a rash all over his body, but refused to give in! 'The doctor told me not to dance and I said, "You don't understand I HAVE to dance!"' the brave newsreader revealed.

Best and worst for each dance ...

Cha Cha Cha: *Best* Jill Halfpenny and Louisa Lytton (36), *Worst* Quentin Willson (8)

Jive: *Best* Jill Halfpenny (40), *Worst* Fiona Phillips (16)

Rumba: *Best* Zoe Ball (38), *Worst* Fiona Phillips (11)

Paso Doble: *Best* Jill Halfpenny and Emma Bunton (37), *Worst* Dennis Taylor and Christopher Parker (15)

Samba: *Best* Zoe Ball (38), *Worst* Christopher Parker (15)

Waltz: *Best* Matt Dawson (38), *Worst* Fiona Phillips (11)

Quickstep: *Best* Darren Gough and Colin Jackson (40), *Worst* Diarmuid Gavin (12)

Foxtrot: *Best* Zoe Ball (38), *Worst* Fiona Phillips (20)

Tango: *Best* Zoe Ball (38), *Worst* Diarmuid Gavin (12)

The
Strictly
Stop
Quiz

How well do you know your Samba from your Salsa? Test your knowledge with this fun Strictly Come Dancing quiz.

1 We know that two sporting heroes have won the competition, but how many took part in the first four series?

2 Who was the first celebrity knocked out of series four?

3 Which celebrity was forced to quit series four on his doctor's advice?

4 What was the name of Julian Clary's masculine alter ego, developed for the Paso Doble?

5 Who are the two married couples among the professional dancers?

6 What did Bruno do to confuse the scorers after Julian Clary and Erin Boag's Jive?

7 What did Lilia lose at the end of her Jive with Matt Dawson?

8 Which famous comedy duo dropped in on Emma Bunton's training session in series four?

9 Which famous sportsman lost out in series three but won the Christmas special?

10 Camilla Dallerup is one of only four dancers to appear in the first four series. Can you name the other three?

11 What was the name of Julian Clary's dog, which he took to every training session?

12 Who was Craig talking to in series three, when he said, 'Man, you can booty shake!'?

13 Which series three contestant is a bee-keeper in his spare time?

14 Izabela's tough teaching methods have landed her which royal nickname?

15 Which dance includes the 'Chicken Walk' and 'Back Rock'?

16 Which dance originally told the story of a lady of the night and her client, or an aloof woman and a smelly gaucho?

17 Whose Austin Powers-style Samba was Len talking about when he said, 'The hideousness of the performance will haunt my dreams for ever.'?

18 Who said, 'Jill is technically brilliant and Denise is enigmatic and like a film star. Then there's me!'?

19 Which female celebrity did Belinda Carlisle say she had been voting for when she appeared on series four?

20 Who did Bruno compare to a sailing ship on her maiden voyage, saying, 'You start off so majestic and then you get a bit of engine trouble.'?

21 What did Quentin Willson wear on his back in the first show of series two?

22 Which generous soul complimented the judges when she was kicked out, saying, 'I love them all and not many people say that, so thank you.'?

23 Where does Brendan Cole come from originally?

24 Which celebrity was knocked out of series two in the semi-finals?

25 Who did reigning champion Darren Bennett partner in series three?

26 Who, according to Arlene, 'ignited her fire'?

27 Which evergreen star was Bruce introducing when he quipped, 'He has such a wonderful voice and he never seems to get a day older. I'm so pleased he's on the show. We have so much in common!'?

28 Who was Len talking to when he joked, 'At one time you snookered your left leg behind your right leg.'?

29 Who partnered James Martin in series three?

30 In which Olympic event did Colin Jackson win a silver medal?

Answers

119

1: Nine (Mark Ramprakash, Matt Dawson, Peter Schmeichel, Martin Offiah, Roger Black, Denise Lewis, Darren Gough, Colin Jackson and Dennis Taylor. **2:** Nicholas Owen **3:** Jimmy Tarbuck **4:** Carlos. **5:** Aleksandra 'Ola' and James Jordan, Darren Bennett and Lilia Kopylova. **6:** He held up a six and seven. **7:** Her earring. **8:** French and Saunders. **9:** Colin Jackson. **10:** Brendan Cole, Anton du Beke and Erin Boag. **11:** Valerie. **12:** Colin Jackson **13:** Bill Turnbull. **14:** Princess of pain. **15:** The Jive. **16:** The Tango. **17:** Christopher Parker and Hanna Karttunen. **18:** Julian Clary. **19:** Louisa Lytton **20:** Jan Ravens. **21:** An L-plate. **22:** Emma Bunton. **23:** New Zealand. **24:** Aled Jones. **25:** Gloria Hunniford. **26:** Mark Ramprakash. **27:** Sir Cliff Richard. **28:** Dennis Taylor. **29:** Camilla Dallerup. **30:** The 110m hurdle.

'I haven't a clue which dance style I'll prefer but I fear for my Latin hip movements '

She may be 60, but there's no doubt Stephanie Beacham will look fabulous in a ball gown. The glamorous granny, and star of *Bad Girls*, says her number one fan is looking forward to her transformation from jailbird to ballroom queen. 'My seven-year-old grandson, Jude, is pleased I'm in the show,' she says. 'He's thrilled that I am not in prison any more and am going to be dancing in pretty outfits instead.'

Stephanie Beacham

Born in Casablanca, Morocco, and brought up in Hertfordshire, Stephanie embarked on her long and successful career as an actress in the 1960s. After travelling to France to study mime under Etienne Decroux, she attended RADA (Royal Academy of Dramatic Art), before taking on various stage roles in the West End.

In 1972, she made her film debut opposite Marlon Brando in *The Nightcomers*, directed by Michael Winner. The moving Second World War drama *Tenko* made her a household name in 1981 and four years later, she landed the most memorable role of her career, as legendary super-bitch Sable Colby in *Dynasty*. More recently, Stephanie starred alongside Amanda Barrie in the popular ITV prison drama *Bad Girls*. The pair played high-class fraudsters Phyllida and Beverley, dubbed the 'Costa Cons', until the show ended in 2006.

The talented actress has a poignant reason for taking part in *Strictly Come Dancing*. 'I recently lost a friend of mine who loved dancing,' she explains. 'I wanted to take part as homage to this person and celebrate their memory.'

Although she studied ballet from the age of four until she was turned down by the Royal Ballet when she was ten, Stephanie has little experience of ballroom. 'My experience consists of standing on my father's feet doing the Waltz when I was five years old,' she laughs.

She was seen on the dance floor as recently as February 2007 – her 60th birthday – doing the pogo by the sounds of it! 'I went to a club in Aberdeen, which was quite a lager lout-y place, and I found myself jumping up and down,' she recalls. 'I remember thinking, "This is rather fun!"'

Although she loves watching the show, she admits she is yet to distinguish between the dances. 'I don't know my Quickstep from my Foxtrot!' she confesses. 'I haven't a clue which dance style I'll prefer but I fear for my Latin hip movements.' And she promises to greet the judges' comments with humour. 'I shall roar with laughter if I am criticised,' she says. 'If I manage to remember a few steps it will be brilliant, so I will not go into a fit of despondency if I get told to put my heels together!'

The elegant star confesses that she was glued to the last series, and was very taken with a certain sportsman. 'All the contestants were fabulous which makes me slightly nervous,' she admits. 'I fell completely in love with Mark, and I think that people with good stamina are the ones that go the distance. The only thing I have stamina for is drinking lots of cups of tea!'

She will be dancing with Vincent Simone

Which Judg

Try our fun quiz and discover which of the judges is most like you.

1 Your husband or partner buys you a bunch of flowers from the petrol station on his way home from work. They are mainly carnations and past their best. Do you say …

a) They're fantastic. That is a lovely gesture.

b) How romantic! You are my very own Romeo and I am your Juliet.

c) That's sweet – but you could have chosen a nicer bunch.

d) Poor effort. Try harder next time.

2 You are choosing a holiday. Do you pick …

a) A shabby flat in the heart of Buenos Aires.

b) White water rafting in Canada.

c) A luxury villa on the French Riviera.

d) Butlins at Bognor.

3 At an expensive restaurant the waiter serves you the house special, which looks beautiful but miniscule. Do you …

a) Send it back and demand something more substantial.

b) Say, 'I need more. Can I have a bowl of chips, please?'

c) Praise the presentation and ignore the rumbling stomach.

d) Say, 'This is like my golf shot … it looks beautiful but fails to fill the hole!'

4 Your best friend has a new dress which is beautiful but deeply unflattering. Do you say…

a) That satin is exquisite and the colour is amazing. Belle of the ball!

b) Did you keep the receipt?

c) Awful. You look like a sumo wrestler in drag.

d) It is a nice dress, but I'm not sure it's your colour.

5 You are making a pudding for a dinner party. Is it …

a) Choux pastry swans wafting in icing sugar on a lake of raspberry coulis.

b) Spotted Dick.

c) Tiramisu.

d) Bitter chocolate and lemon cheesecake.

6 Your partner suggests a camping holiday whereas you fancy a luxury hotel by the sea. Do you say …

a) There's no way I am sleeping in a tent with you and that's final!

b) Camping holidays are very nice but it might rain, the tent is too small and the food is terrible.

c) You are Tarzan and I am Jane! Tarzan may be fine in the jungle but Jane prefers feather beds to soggy ground sheets.

d) Camping's fine with me, as long as we have a beach holiday later.

7 When choosing your ideal car do you go for …

a) A Ferrari.
b) A Mercedes sports.
c) A vintage VW camper van.
d) A Ford Mondeo.

8 Your daughter or niece has drawn you a picture which is terrible, even for her age group. Do you say …

a) That's lovely darling. What is it?
b) The house is good but the little girl needs work and the clouds are the wrong shape.
c) Is that the best you can do?
d) A regular Picasso.

9 A friend is starring in an amateur dramatic production and drags you along. It turns out to be the most boring thing you've ever watched. When he/she asks what you think, do you say …

a) How brave!
b) It started out as Chekhov and ended up as the Chuckle Brothers.
c) Dull, dull, dull!
d) I didn't pick up any sexual tension and the drama was missing.

10 Which of the following shows are you most likely to go and see?

a) *West Side Story*.
b) *Singin' in the Rain*.
c) *Chicago*.
d) *Les Miserables*.

Count up your points and find how you scored?

1: a)1 b)2 c)3 d)4 **2:** a)2 b)4 c)3 d)1 **3:** a)4 b)3 c)2 d)1 **4:** a)2 b)3 c)4 d)1 **5:** a)3 b)1 c)3 d)4 **6:** a)4 b)3 c)2 d)1 **7:** a)2 b)3 c)4 d)1 **8:** a)1 b)3 c)4 d)2 **9:** a)1 b)2 c)4 d)3 **10:** a)2 b)1 c)3 d)4

1-11: Len

You are a traditionalist who likes things done a certain way and are not too keen on change. Nonetheless, you are kind and recognise the effort that people put in, always focusing on their good points before being openly critical.

12-21: Bruno

Passion, romance and flourish are the things that win you over and you love a good drama. Humdrum doesn't do for you! But you choose your words carefully when dealing with others and will flamboyantly praise the things you see as beautiful or good.

22-31: Arlene

Elegance and style are your watchwords and you are quite sure you deserve the best! You seek beauty and refection in everything and there's nothing wrong with that, but sometimes your sharp tongue can be more cutting than your friends would like.

32-40: Craig

Ouch! You say it like it is and take no prisoners on the way! You love things that are creative, edgy and slightly off the beaten track and you will always stand out from a crowd. But blunt speaking can be very hurtful to those around you.

Dennis Taylor may have been snookered by the Paso Doble in series three, but that doesn't stop friend and fellow player Willie Thorne having a shot at the title. And Craig had better be kind to the record-breaking snooker player. 'When Dennis challenged Craig to learn to play snooker in five days, I took part in his lessons,' recalls Willie. 'If Craig comments about my dancing, I'm going to gently remind him how rubbish he was at snooker!'

Willie Thorne

Willie started playing snooker at the age of 14, in the club where his dad worked as a steward. Currently the World Seniors Snooker Champion, he has gained a total of 14 tournament victories worldwide and was a regular in the top 16 world ranking players for over a decade. He also holds the record for the highest number of maximum breaks in the history of the game, with 190.

Over his 25-year career, he has become a well-loved personality and has appeared on numerous TV shows, including *Big Break*, *Noel's House Party* and *A Question of Sport*. More recently, he has turned commentator for all of the major snooker championships on Sky TV, ITV and the BBC.

Now the Great WT, as he is affectionately known, is up for a new challenge – and a chance to trim the waistline. 'I am a glutton for punishment,' laughs the 53-year-old. 'Even though I can't dance, I've never tried to learn, so I thought I would give it a go. I'm also hoping it might help me to lose some weight!'

Willie attends many functions, often as an after-dinner speaker, and he usually gets up for a slow dance, but admits that he can only manage a few steps – and even that doesn't always go smoothly. At one function, he was dancing with a lady, when he trod on her dress and ripped it!

His favourite dance memory is his first dance with wife Jill at their wedding four years ago, but he is quite anxious about his first dance on *SCD*. 'I worry about falling over on live television and I also don't want to be the first male celebrity to be eliminated. Then again, I'm afraid of getting through the first round because of what is going to follow!'

He will be dancing with Erin Boag

As a sportsman, though, he is in it to win it – but doesn't hold out a lot of hope. 'I am a very competitive person and usually *have* to win at all costs, but I'm not sure I can win this competition,' he says. 'I think every other competitor would have to fall over for that to happen!' At least Willie can count on plenty of family support as he and Jill, who live in Leicester, have five children between them. And he'll definitely get on well with Bruce – he has a passion for golf and plays off a handicap of ten. So, if he doesn't impress the judges with his American Smooth, he's sure to impress Bruce with his swing.

'I'm not sure I can win this competition. I think every other competitor would have to fall over for that to happen!'

		Alesha & Matthew	Brian & Karen	Gabby & James	Dominic & Lilia	Kate & Anton	Gethin & Camilla	Kelly & Brendan	
Show 1	Your Score								
	Judges' Score								
Show 2	Your Score								
	Judges' Score								
Show 3	Your Score								
	Judges' Score								
Show 4	Your Score								
	Judges' Score								
Show 5	Your Score								
	Judges' Score								
Show 6	Your Score								
	Judges' Score								
Show 7	Your Score								
	Judges' Score								
Show 8	Your Score								
	Judges' Score								
Show 9	Your Score								
	Judges' Score								
Show 10	Your Score								
	Judges' Score								
Show 11	Your Score								
	Judges' Score								
The Final	Your Score								
	Judges' Score								

	John & Nicole	Letitia & Darren	Kenny & Ola	Penny & Ian	Matt & Flavia	Stephanie & Vincent	Willie & Erin	Knocked Out
								Winner

You Dancin'?

IMPERIAL SOCIETY OF TEACHERS OF DANCING

The ISTD Dance Examinations Board offers dance examinations in 15 dance genres, including Modern Ballroom and Latin-American. Teachers who offer their examinations can be found throughout the UK and overseas. If you can't find a teacher in your area they will provide a list of schools, just email: education@istd.org.

Imperial House
22–6 Paul Street
London EC2A 4QE

Tel: +44 (0)20 7377 1577
Website: www.istd.org

NATIONAL ASSOCIATION OF TEACHERS OF DANCING

The National Association offers classes and examinations in the following branches: Ballroom, Latin-American, Disco, Street, Rock 'n' Roll, Country & Western Line Dancing, Salsa, Mambo, Merengue, Classical & Modern Sequence. Contact them for more information.

NATD
44–7 The Broadway
Thatcham
Berkshire RG19 3HP

Tel: + 44 (0) 1635 868888
Website: www.natd.org.uk

INTERNATIONAL DANCE TEACHERS' ASSOCIATION

Log on to their website to find a dance teacher or course near you – all over the world – or contact them direct and they will send you a free and comprehensive list of IDTA-registered teachers in your area.

International House
76 Bennett Road
Brighton
East Sussex BN2 5JL

Tel: +44 (0)1273 685652
Website: www.idta.co.uk

UNITED KINGDOM ALLIANCE OF PROFESSIONAL TEACHERS OF DANCING

Log on to their website or contact the UKA direct for guidance on finding your nearest registered dance teacher.

Centenary House
38–40 Station Road
Blackpool
FY4 1EU

Tel: +44 (0)1253 408828
Website: www.ukadance.co.uk